# Reasons to Believe

# Reasons to Believe

## A Journey of Spiritual Awareness

### in the Modern World

## Robert Lefavi, PhD

Hope Publishing House
Pasadena, California

For information address:
**Hope Publishing House**
P.O. Box 60008
Pasadena, CA 91116 - U.S.A.
Tel: (626) 792-6123 / Fax: (626) 792-2121
Visa/MC orders to: (800) 326-2671
E-mail: hopepub@loop.com
Web site: http://www.hope-pub.com
Cover design — Michael McClary/The Workshop

Printed on acid-free paper

**Library of Congress Cataloging-in-Publication Data**

Lefavi, Robert, 1960-
    Reasons to believe : a journey of spiritual awareness in the modern world /
by Robert Lefavi.
       p.   cm.
    Includes bibliographical references.
    ISBN 0-932727-44-1
    1. Religion and science. 2. Spirituality. I. Title
BT1220.L44  1999
   291.1'75--dc21                                 99-21587
                                                     CIP

For Sue,

*my greatest blessing*

# Table of Contents

# Preface/Acknowledgments

When we are open to grace, we find that people appear in our lives
who encourage the growth of souls.                    —Joan Borysenko

I have dreamt of the day I would put this book in your hands. It
is the culmination of my search for the essence of true spirituality, one
I am convinced was initiated by the grace of God.

A great spiritual movement is under way in Western society,
launched by people who honestly seek to reconnect to the cornerstone
of their spiritual awareness—that which is divine. Unfortunately, many
spiritually-minded people in contemporary society have difficulty reconciling their spiritual life with what science and the modern world describe as real. Too many educated people feel they have to check their
brains at the door when entering a church, synagogue or mosque.

Moreover, many powerful influences hinder people in contemporary society from seeing with spiritual eyes, creating a spiritual denial
both within their souls and within society. Can we break out of this
paradigm? Yes, but only after we recognize these spiritually-stifling influences can we awaken our "spiritual sense" and bring about personal
and social change.

In *Reasons to Believe* I contend that, in the modern world, people
often need a validation of their inner awareness of God on a level they
have been accustomed to and can comprehend—science and reason. I
have found that when this occurs, they are then able to awaken their
spirituality and subsequently open up to the mystery of the divine and
live more fully. A new life begins—one filled with joy, peace and things

eternal. (It is after encountering "reasons to believe" and beginning a process of spiritual growth that people realize they never needed any validation at all – it was always within them).

If you are a thinking person struggling to reconcile your spiritual longing with the secular world and seeking a deeper level of reality, then this book is for you. Here you'll find the ground-breaking, fascinating harmony existing between contemporary scientific findings and spiritual tenets – a discovery I describe in the context of my inner and outer spiritual search. While many books are available examining the consistency between spiritual tenets and natural science, health and medicine, or social issues, here I also discuss (a) how all three areas support our spiritual sense, and (b) the personal and social damage brought on by the pervasive denial of God and our spirituality in the age of science.

During my research many individuals have facilitated my growth – some wittingly, some unwittingly. Drs. M. Scott Peck, Paul Pearsall, Tom Deters, H. Tom Ford, James Repella, Sandy Streater, along with Fr. Michael Dufault, Rev. Derek McAleer, Mr. Brian Welch, Mr. Douglas Smith, Mr. Steve Blechman and Mr. Gene Johnston have all been instrumental in enabling my transition from body-building to spirit-building. Special thanks to Ms. Christina Van Dyke, MA, for her editing and counsel, to Rev. Ralph Bailey for showing me the incredible compassion necessary in any search for spiritual "truth," and to my students, many of whom have taught me at least as much as I have taught them. Most of all, I thank my parents – Lucy Del Toro Lefavi and the late Thomas E. Lefavi – for showing me what love is.

In *Reasons to Believe*, I define spirituality early on and distinguish it from religion, yet others I quoted might use the terms "spirituality" and "religion" interchangeably and may have different meanings for them. May the material herein ignite your awareness of God's inner call to you today.

*–Robert Lefavi, PhD*
*Savannah, GA*

# 1

# Knowledge of the Spirit

Seek not abroad, turn back into thyself, for in the inner [person] dwells the truth. — St. Augustine

The heart has its reasons of which reason knows nothing.... It is the heart which perceives God and not the reason. That is what faith is: God perceived by the heart, not by the reason. — 17th century French mathematician Blaise Pascal

I do not now, nor will I ever, believe in God.

You see, to "believe" in something requires one to make a conscious choice to accept the existence of that entity, often at the expense of the existence of at least one other entity, each displaying some evidence (empirical, theoretical or anecdotal) of being.

For example, I *believe* that forgiveness is necessary for true healing to occur in damaged relationships because my research has consistently shown me so; I am convinced of it, but I could be wrong. Likewise, I used to believe in the Easter Bunny because my parents told me about this benevolent rabbit that left chocolate candy at Easter. Oftentimes, upon the discovery of additional evidence, we discard old beliefs for new ones.

Thus, it would not be truthful for me to say that I believe in God. You see, I *know* there is a God. Absolutely no other possible reality exists other than that of an almighty power who created and directs the universe. This is not a belief of mine; it is *knowledge* I have.

Of course, upon hearing this, people often ask, "Well, *how* do you *know* God exists?" The only way I can respond to those who ask such a question is to tell them in all sincerity that the very fact that they have asked this means there is no way they could possibly understand or be satisfied with my answer.

No, this is *not* a cop-out; my knowledge of God's existence is a function of the deepest parts of my mind, body and spirit knowing God. My "evidence" is spiritual, rather than empirical, theoretical or anecdotal, yet its validity permeates every cell of my body in a manner more real and intense than any other truth I have ever known. Clearly, if you have not or do not experience this spiritual knowledge, no one could adequately describe its reality to you.

One's knowledge and understanding of God takes place in the "soul," or in what French mathematician and religious thinker Blaise Pascal referred to as "the heart" (as in the quote above)—that inner domain where the spirit sees with eyes of truth. However, if you have proceeded down the difficult path leading toward spiritual knowledge and enlightenment, that God exists is the only thing of which you can truly be certain.

Further, this knowledge of God is not a *choice* I make between possibilities; rather it is a recognition of what has been, is, and always will be. It is a part of my being, the essence of my eternal self. Likewise, while deep within my soul I have always "known" the reality of God, its more recent emergence from my core is as much a *remembrance* as it is an *awakening*.

If you think there is at least some similarity between what I have described here and your personal interests, then this book will help you illuminate your spiritual path. You see, I am certain that we all have the potential, and many the inner longing, to awaken to this knowledge of the spirit.

## Reawakened

When the student is ready the teacher appears.
— Zen proverb

Less than a decade ago I was a poster child for the material world. In fact, you couldn't have created a more secular, nonspiritual person than me if you tried. Here's the person I was.

As a doctoral student at Auburn University in Alabama, I was training to be a research scientist in an academic setting. It was clear to me early in my course of study, as I'm sure it is to most graduate students in the sciences, that if I was to survive in the "publish or perish" academic environment, the only thing that really mattered was what I could measure and prove. Thus, my potential for success, with my self-worth not far behind, was intimately tied to physical proof. That which was felt, no matter how compelling, was relatively insignificant.

Second, I was a competitive bodybuilder and power-lifter of some national prominence. While I was certainly far from being a sports superstar, I won my share of titles, made a good living giving seminars on physique development, was featured in a nice collection of magazine articles, and was flattered with more than a few autograph requests. Like many who compete in high-level athletics, I easily got caught up in a life filled with mirrors, money, materialism and "me."

Only now can I look back and get a good laugh at myself. It is rather ironic that I was successful in the sport of body-building because I was able to create an appealing aesthetic illusion with my physique; only later would I see that, in a certain sense, it was all an illusion. Once again, though, my worth was vested in that which was physical – how I looked, how muscular my arms were, and so on.

Third, and of significance to everyone close to middle age, I was a product of the Baby-Boom generation. Like any certified Boomer, I distrusted organized anything and as I shed the establishment of religion, with it went everything I associated with my spirituality.

Additionally, I placed great value on my ability to carve a unique, new path according to my own determination of what was important. However, when I saw my contemporaries getting involved in New Age nonsense, I became even more turned off to "spirituality" and sank deeper into what the world valued as "real." (Later, I would see this New Age "spirituality" as a secular form, not true spirituality.)

Finally, I watched my father, whom I considered to be the last of the "good" guys, die a slow, often painful death. A just God who's involved in our lives? Not from what I could see.

Yep, a poster boy for materialism, that was I – and totally asleep to my own true spiritual self.

## A Helping Hand

Then, something strange happened in 1992. I can still feel it as if it were yesterday. It might sound more than a bit odd to you, but I swear on my life it occurred.

In the middle of the night, I awoke aware that there was a hand touching me in the middle of my back. That's right, a hand simply resting on my back. I felt paralyzed, but I honestly was not afraid. Within a few seconds, the hand was gone just as it came. (It didn't "leave." It was just gone.) At that moment, I looked up quickly and asked my wife, "Sue, was that you?"

She was out like a light. Besides, I knew it wasn't Sue; the hand was much too large and facing the wrong way for her to have put either of her hands on my back. I stayed up the rest of the night assuring myself I wasn't crazy. Soon, not being able to make sense of this extraordinary occurrence, I slowly put it out of my mind. Only later, as I looked back on what was clearly a pivotal time in my life, did I remember that event, realizing the many unusual things that began to happen after that incident.

For example, it seems more than coincidental that after that night I rather suddenly became fascinated with the question of creation—a topic I hadn't given much thought to in at least a decade. But now, for some reason, the entire creation issue was bothering me. I felt compelled to call a friend of mine, Dr. Joe Chromiak, a researcher at Brown University's Miriam Hospital and a person I knew was very spiritual so he wouldn't mind being quizzed about God and science. I scribbled notes as fast as I could while Joe rattled off theories, scripture, books and authors, adding, "Gee, Bob, I didn't know you were into this stuff!"

I remember responding, "I'm not, or I wasn't—until now."

Just as I was satisfying my need to study creation anew, I began questioning the latest findings in health science (my field of study), identifying all the clear relations between spirituality and health. I gathered research project upon research project on the aspects of spirituality that play a role in conventional medicine and optimal health.

I began buying and reading every book on the sciences I could get my hands on that even remotely alluded to spirituality. Since science was the only thing I was trained to believe was real, this frame of reference gave me the security I needed at the beginning of my search. I reasoned that if scientists addressed these issues, then I couldn't be too far out there with my newfound interests.

Sue would routinely take people into my study just so they could get a good chuckle at the stacks of books piled so high I could barely work. I discussed my questions with spiritual people who were seeking God anyplace and everyplace from monasteries to synagogues and I had an unquenchable desire to reconcile the truths I was confronting with everything I had always accepted to be true about the world.

Soon I came to realize that in many cases I could not have concrete answers, so I sought out learned people who would at least help me identify the right questions. What does spiritual growth entail? Is belief in the Bible's creation account completely at odds with science's explanation of the origin of the universe and life? Can one's spirituality affect the body? Why do bad things happen to good people? Will this journey undo all my scientific training or, worse yet, will it turn me into a pretentious, holier-than-thou evangelist?

I felt as if I were on a mission.

Unfortunately, not everyone was receptive to hearing about my personal journey. When I began to talk about spirituality in my profession as a professor of health science, I was met with objections and warnings that academia was not the place for it. This was an inappropriate pursuit, I was told by some, while others added that to infer anything about God from science was nonsense. You see, even though academia is supposed to be an environment of free thinking, open minds, it's much easier for people to pigeonhole your ideas into whatever they can relate it to than to try to analyze objectively what you're saying. Undaunted by this disappointment, I continued my search for knowledge and answers to life's ultimate spiritual concerns.

To be sure, the pull of the material world is still strong and the person I am now hasn't forgotten the old "Bob." No doubt I'm only a few stupid decisions away from being the intelligent fool I was. Yet, it's as if I'm visualizing another person when I think of my former self, so different am I from that empty shell.

Only now do I see those surrounding me in my former life for what they truly represented and how they influenced me: athletes who were idolized by many, yet were wrecks personally and spiritually; rich men who feared death so much they surrounded themselves with reminders of their importance (often young women and big toys); and scientists who couldn't see past their microscopes.

It's as if my life is somehow now in the process of *fulfillment* and I've returned to the spiritually-aware person God meant me to be. I also feel a sense of freedom from the straightjacket of person-made religion, pompous science and blind secularism, having found my way back to the essence of spirituality.

I sincerely believe I needed to experience *exactly* what I have gone through to appreciate fully my spirituality. Soulbuilding made perfect sense only after I saw the superficiality and fruitlessness of body-building and material-building. Had God, by grace, prodded me – as I believe God did – without my early false perspective, I probably couldn't have recognized my estrangement from God, even when God, by grace, prodded me. So my material focus was, paradoxically, the soil in which my quiet inner longing to be reconnected to God could take root and sprout.

Did the hand that touched me bring about my metamorphosis? I don't know, but I believe it did. I know only that after that strange night in 1992, the fire of the divine within my soul was kindled; my sense of spirituality, which was longing to be recognized, was awakened. I am certain that others as well desire to rekindle their spirituality. Now, more than ever, the world is made up of a large percentage of "thinkers" who are reëvaluating old truths and paradigms. Additionally, feelings of meaninglessness and purposelessness have become prevalent among all people, and many are looking for spiritual fulfillment, seeking a return to that which is truly real.

I also believe events regularly happen to all of us which can act as calls to a spiritual awakening. Clearly, each of us has multiple opportunities to connect to our often-buried knowledge of God. While my purpose in life may not be the same as anyone else's, we all – consciously or subconsciously – make the choice either to ignore or pursue calls to spiritual awareness.

For me, my life now makes sense. Actually, to some degree, I'd say my life makes perfect sense. I feel as if God has been directing me in a play all along and now I'm finally getting a chance to understand my part. The peace that accompanies this realization is indescribable.

I thank God for helping me find my way back to an inner knowledge of God. Perhaps by describing in this book what I discovered during my search and journey, including things that both *clarified* and *clouded* my awareness of and relationship with God, I might help you become aware of your spiritual knowledge of God. At the least, you might begin to recognize God's gentle – and sometimes not so gentle – prodding toward spiritual awareness. Only after this awareness occurs can you grow spiritually and reach your full potential as a whole human being.

# The "Spiritual Sense"

. . . according to the measure of faith that God has assigned.
                    – in St. Paul's letter to the Romans (12:3)

The intelligence that allows us to appreciate the nature of
God and also the nature of the universe that God created,
I'm sure, is very much a part of God's plan . . . We have the
mental capacities to image the world and to image God.
                    – Religious philosopher Dr. Nancey Murphy

Deep inside me, there lay hidden a shining spark, which
seemed to be waiting for an opportunity to flame up brightly
and freely.                    – Abbess Thaisia of Leushino,
                    spiritual daughter of St. John of Kronstadt

I have come to call the spiritual knowledge that I believe is
imprinted in every part of my – and your – being our "spiritual
sense." Unlike our other five senses, our spiritual sense is
anchored in the spirit and soul (emotions, mind and will). Over
the centuries others have referred to this type of intuition or
instinct in different ways.

The spiritual sense is related to what the early 17th-century
French philosopher René Descartes would refer to as humankind's "God-consciousness" in his *ontological* argument for the
existence of God. Descartes believed that humankind's *ideas* of
God imply the existence of a God who would imprint such
ideas in us (God would want us to be able to conceive of God
and know God). In other words, because we can think of God
as a perfect and necessary being, therefore God exists; God gave
us such a consciousness! How else would we all have such a
universal idea of God? Likewise, St. Augustine saw God as
being eternal truth and believed that we already know God by
having a little bit of this eternal truth within us.

In addition, it's interesting that even some of today's mainstream scientists are becoming more comfortable addressing the

spiritual sense, the seed of one's spirituality. Thus, after 30 years of scientific research, Harvard physician Herbert Benson has concluded that we are "wired for God," and are all built to engage in and exercise our spiritual beliefs. Benson's assertion has at least anecdotal support in that a sense of a higher power and one's spirituality is common among people of every culture known to humankind.

## Spiritual Growth in America

As I discuss this spiritual sense at various speaking engagements throughout the country, I am encouraged that more and more people are becoming aware of their inner knowledge of the divine and are more in tune with their spirituality. When I listen closely to those who describe their spiritual journeys, I realize that this sense manifests itself at different times in various ways to bring about spiritual awareness and initiate one's growth and development.

Slowly but surely, more Americans are paying attention to their inner knowledge of that which is spiritual. For example, the popular new field of "noetics" (derived from the Greek word "nous," literally meaning all-encompassing ways of knowing) includes the use of spiritual as well as scientific knowledge in its definition of reality. Noetics is growing at an exponential rate and seems to touch the core of a person, because it gives credence not only to that which one can see, but also that which is felt deep within the soul.

This is important because, as I have experienced and as I will contend throughout this book, only when we become aware of our inner knowledge of the divine can the spiritual self grow in the direction of its potential. How difficult this becomes in the modern world that's dominated by science where the only things that count are those that can be counted.

Unfortunately, despite this slow resurgence of our spiritual selves intrapersonally, a concurrent social phenomenon prevails where Americans avoid discussing spiritual truths and will only deal with spiritual *relativism,* presumably so that no one is offended. Case in point are the "value clarification exercises" in school curricula which often focus on helping students identify their values so at least they know what they think is right.

My personal journey has convinced me that there *are* spiritual truths, that Americans *are* genuinely interested in them and ready to involve this wisdom more fully in their lives. George Gallup's mid-1990s poll which identified "the search for spiritual moorings" as a "dominant trend," gives me more confidence in my belief. In this search, however, we must realize that we cannot seek personal spiritual growth and subsequent societal change without limitations until we recognize and awaken our spiritual sense.

The time is right for Americans to embrace wholeheartedly their spirituality, the only part of themselves that is truly real.

## Dimensions of Spirituality

> Great [people] are they who see that the spiritual is stronger
> than any material force.          –Ralph Waldo Emerson

I have found that often the word *spirituality* is itself a "hot button," subject to much misinterpretation. So first let me clarify what I mean when I use the term, though I believe my definition is consistent with those of many others.

Spirituality (from the Latin *spiritus* which means "breath of life") is the nonphysical and nonmental aspect of a person; a force or spirit that is the *transcendent* essence of an individual as well the source of unity and meaning in that person. It is the "foreverness" of ourselves. I have become convinced that an awakening to our spiritual selves brings about a commitment directing us toward the ultimate values of love, purpose, truth and goodness.

Because this can sometimes sound like a lot of mumbo-jumbo let me provide some structure to this definition. As a result of my research, I have designed two *dimensions* of spirituality, each having five *subdimensions.* These specific dimensions and subdimensions often help people get a better handle on what is meant by spirituality in an applied sense.

The first dimension is *Belief in a Higher Power* (here I use "belief" as it is conventionally used). I also call this the *vertical* dimension because it focuses on a higher power. Within this dimension are the subdimensions of:

- *Creed*
- *Hope, optimism and patience*
- *Belief in an afterlife*
- *Purpose in life*
- *Transcendence*

One's inner feelings and outward expression of *Love and Goodness* are the second dimension of spirituality. I call this the horizontal dimension as it highlights one's feelings, practices and actions in the world. (When I describe the vertical and horizontal dimensions to Christians, they naturally see spirituality as a "cross.") Within this dimension are the subdimensions of:

- *Deed*
- *Love and Connection*
- *Humility*
- *Forgiveness*
- *Worship, prayer, or meditation*

*Clarifying Creed and Transcendence*

In the first dimension, two subdimensions occasionally require clarification. Creed, or belief in the divine, is the most

12                                        Reasons to Believe

*fundamental* and important dimension of spirituality. That is, an understanding that a higher power exists is the *necessary* component of spirituality. Unequivocally, God is the key to our spirituality. In fact, the *American Heritage Dictionary of the English Language* (1992) defines "spiritual" as "of, from or relating to God." Thus, when we deny God, we deny our spirituality, and vice versa.

I am still occasionally asked about spirituality without God. This is impossible; it's an oxymoron. I have often heard someone say things like, "I don't really believe in God but I consider myself a spiritual person" – a contradiction in terms. To be focused on spirituality necessitates an awareness of and a longing for that which is greater than humans and only possible with a higher power – order, grace, love, purpose, beauty and so on (what Plato would call the "intelligible" things).

One popular contemporary "spiritual" movement is what I call "secular spirituality." This form of spirituality, I contend, is not spirituality at all because it focuses on the power of humankind, not God. There seems to be no *creed* or belief, except in the self. Secular spirituality is a fraud; it's a "you-can-do-anything-if-you-just-reconnect-to-your-hidden-power" charade. The modern world has facilitated an estrangement of people from their spiritual selves for so long they don't even know what spirituality is anymore. As author Jacob Needleman says, "We live such constricted lives that the slightest triggering of a new vital energy gets labeled 'spiritual'."

Another concept that's difficult to grasp is "transcendence." It refers to the ability to extend ourselves beyond our immediate context to achieve new perspectives. Many people feel they transcend their place and time when they have "peak experiences." They may feel a sense of awe and timelessness. As personal examples of this awe, I feel transcendence when I dwell on the eternal nothingness that would exist without God and the immensity of the cosmos God created. Self-transcendence can also be felt in art, music, religion, the sharing of legacies, and so forth.

Often people confuse the subdimension of transcendence with spirituality itself. When we stand at the edge of the Grand Canyon we may briefly glimpse God's immense power and appreciate with awe what God has created. At that moment we may also feel we transcend space and time. While we may look at this as a spiritual experience, it is not the beginning and end of our spirituality – God is. Without God, there is nothing to transcend to, no other power to commune with. Thus God enables us to transcend, to appreciate God and to feel a sense of awe at God's power. In fact, Plato and St. Augustine referred to transcendence as the soul catching a glimpse of God, seeing God's perfection.

*Clarifying Deed and the Love Connection*

The second dimension of spirituality, that of Love and Goodness, also contains two subdimensions that frequently need defining – deed and connection.

While creed, one's actual belief in the divine, is a necessary component of spirituality, deed exercises and promotes one's spiritual growth. Essentially, deed refers to outward expressions of goodness – altruism, charity and kindness – and our desire for that which is good, happiness and morality.

I once had the honor of bringing a powerful and famous man to an important community event. Most people, having seen and heard this person on television, would immediately assume he is a spiritually-based person and would ascribe to him characteristics of kindness and compassion – even on a bad day. Although he was polite to me, I was floored by how rude, unkind and mean-spirited he was to nearly everyone who happened to be in his path. Still, his actions were mostly ignored and he was treated like a king because he was who he was.

While traveling home from the event I attended with this person, I remembered a poor, elderly woman I would occasionally meet at a store in rural eastern Alabama when commuting to my doctoral classes. She was angelic, had a warm, pleasant smile and always an act of kindness or a kind word for someone. You couldn't leave her store without her serenade, "God bless you, chil'." Your spirit was lifted when you met her.

Not only would I argue that the *choice* this woman, of whom I'm certain you will never hear, made to be kind and good to others rendered her more spiritually advanced than the famous person I encountered, but I would also suggest that it gave her the happiness and success in life few people find. Her good deeds, not fame or money, set her apart from others.

Finally, the subdimension of love and connection refers to the extent that intimacy, belonging and closeness is fostered in one's life. Being "connected" to a person or group is a universal need where one cares for and communes with other people. Often, loving, connected individuals have a desire to solve social problems and focus on the spiritual growth of others.

Through an understanding of the dimensions of spirituality, one sees that spirituality is completely and mutually exclusive from power, intelligence, fame and financial or social status. In fact, my discussions on spirituality with thousands of people have convinced me that those with more of the above might even be at a disadvantage when developing their spiritual selves. Frequently the feelings of self-worth in the powerful, rich and famous can become so closely tied to and vested in what society tells them is real – more money, power and fame – that they get caught up in a cycle of having to continue the construction and maintenance of a material self at the expense of a spiritual self.

However, because of the seed of divine knowledge God has

placed in all of us, there is hope for every person. In the modern world, this hope rests on the events in our lives that bring about the potential to awaken to our spiritual selves and our eternal knowledge of God.

## Spirituality and Religion

Spirituality has to do with experience; religion has to do with the conceptualization of that experience. Spirituality focuses on what happens in the heart; religion tries to codify and capture that experience in a system.  – Thomas Legere

At the beginning of my return to God, it was important for me to distinguish between the sense of spirituality to which I was awakening and organized religion. It was comforting to find that spirituality is not religion per se, but rather is at the core of all major religions. Religious doctrines are typically tools for spiritual growth, means to an end, so to speak. Keep in mind, however, that tools can be used correctly or incorrectly. One can be very religious with little sense of spirituality, and – although it may be more difficult – one may be very spiritual with little knowledge of religious doctrine.

In addition, religion often depends upon an organized faith with a set of dogma; whereas true spirituality focuses on a personal communication with the divine, without influence of formal organization or dogma. (I do not mean to denigrate dogma; it is only harmful when it is used to separate people from God.) Further contrasting the two, a spiritual sense and relationship with the divine exists regardless of the awareness of the individual, while religion requires the awareness of the individual.

I have come to believe that your religious membership, if you have one, should be a private matter; your spirituality, on the other hand, should be more a public matter and may even be a social necessity. Moreover, spirituality focuses on the message while religion concentrates on rituals, traditions and specific historic events. ("Religion" comes from the Latin *religio* which originally meant "form of worship" – ritual, prayer and other outward signs of faith.) I have heard others propose, and I somewhat see their point, that religion is for people who are trying to avoid hell while spirituality is for those who've already been there!

Let me state emphatically that I'm not against organized religion. Clearly, religious worship in a place where people congregate is the most common vehicle used to grow spiritually and to express one's spirituality. What is unfortunate, I believe, is that for many people the potential usefulness of religion as a tool for spiritual growth is eclipsed by its baggage – its problems of the past and present.

For instance, on an almost daily basis we hear of people killing one another and performing acts of violence in the name of religion. The absurdity of this is even more apparent when we consider that violence, even to protect or defend one's organized religion, was not and is not the preferred method to handle conflict in any body of scripture.

In fact, nowhere in the ancient Bible does the word "religion" appear. Even Jesus of Nazareth refrained from saying anything like, "I've come to bring you religion," or "I want to make you a religious people." (Rather, he said, "I am come that they might have life, and that they might have it more abundantly" Jn 10:10.)

We must remember that humankind, not God, created organized religion. As psychiatrist M. Scott Peck, author of *The Road Less Traveled,* has written, this baggage of terrible acts comes from things we have done to God, not things God has done to us.

Yet I don't think religion, with all its dogma, rituals and traditions could avoid many of these problems. Organized religion has attempted to provide a structure for spiritual expression and by virtue of that rigid structure has created something it may not be able to fully control.

## Stages of Spiritual Growth

> We are not human beings having a spiritual experience; we are spiritual beings having a human experience.
> — Teilhard de Chardin

Whether one's spirituality is expressed in a religious setting or in complete solitude, the goal of any spiritual pursuit is continued growth that will ultimately result in a close personal relationship or "communion" with God. Just as there are stages of physical and psychological growth, so there are stages of spiritual growth. Scholars have attempted to conceptualize and define this growth through models. As you read through the three popular models of spiritual growth that follow, notice the similarities between them.

James Fowler discusses faith across one's lifespan in his groundbreaking book *Stages of Faith.* Fowler finds the stages of spiritual growth are similar for all people. The first stage, Primal faith, is characterized by the kind of faith and trust infants possess when separated from their parents. This gives way to Intuitive-Projective faith, which is focused on external authorities and the display of power. In the next stage, Mythic-Literal faith, one views the religious stories of trusted persons as absolute; beliefs and morals are held concretely and literally.

With further growth, one moves into Synthetic-Conventional faith in which "truths" from significant persons are synthesized and authorities are chosen. Next, Individuating-Reflexive faith pushes one to challenge long-held beliefs and recognize personal responsibility for one's life and environment. In the next stage of Paradoxical-Consolidative faith one acknowledges the validity and truth in spiritual claims other than one's own. This is an important step as a person maintains commitments while honoring and respecting those of others. Finally, upon further growth, one moves toward Universalizing faith, in which a person dwells in the world as a transforming presence. Here one's community is universal and inclusive, ready for fellowship with anyone.

Psychiatrist M. Scott Peck also believes that human spiritual development follows a clear, predictable pattern. In fact, Peck has reformed Fowler's seven-stage model, condensing it into four stages of growth. In Peck's model, one starts in the Chaotic/ Antisocial stage where spirituality is absent and persons are unprincipled, yet they pretend to be loving. Often people in this stage are self-serving and manipulative. The second stage, in which one depends on institutions for governance (prison, military, church, business organizations, certain forms of religion, etc.), Peck calls the Formal/Institutional stage. A person in this stage may be attracted to fundamentalist religions. Upon further growth, one moves into the Skeptic/Individual stage. Here one seeks truth, questions everything and looks for alternative ways to explore one's spirituality. Finally, in the Mystical/Communal stage, a person sees the cohesion beneath all things and desires unity and community. In this stage, one is perfectly comfortable with paradox and mysteries – things need not be cut and dried, questions need not have answers at all.

Interestingly, Jane Loevinger's ego development model corresponds well with Fowler's and Peck's models. After all, ego development is, at its core, a spiritual process. Loevinger's model starts with one's behavior being focused on the exploitation and manipulation of others. People see "morality" in terms of what will get them short-term results. Loevinger calls those in the next stage "conformists" because they seek companionship with those who fit narrowly stereotyped and conventional standards of appropriateness. The conformist is preoccupied with materialism, reputation and status. Next, the "self-aware" person evaluates group standards, becomes aware of multiple possibilities in situations and sees that truths may not be so rigid and absolute. Loevinger calls the next stage, in which one tends to acknowledge one's own failures, has great concern for communication and community and sees oneself as the origin of one's personal destiny, the "conscientious" stage.

In the next, "individualistic," stage of development, one is aware of individuality and personal development and has an increased tolerance for contradiction and paradox. People then move into the "autonomous" stage, where they cope well with inner conflicts, ambiguity and the integration of seemingly incompatible ideas. A person in this stage allows others to choose their own paths and make their own mistakes; self-fulfillment is highly valued. In the last of Loevinger's stages one reaches the "integrated" level. Here, a person reconciles conflicts, cherishes differences and contradictions and develops a sense of identity where personal limitations are recognized and fully accepted.

These three models can be laid one atop another as they seem to describe the same general process of spiritual growth, whether from a theological (Fowler), psychiatric (Peck), or psychological (Loevinger) point of view. Clearly, there is a common theme running through them which describes a person's spiritual growth as moving from an instinctive and non-principled level to an externally-oriented level where others provide direction, to a level where truths are explored, to one in which tolerance manifests and finally to a level of mystical unity and connectedness with all.

Spiritual growth, however, does not occur in a vacuum.

During our daily lives, we are constantly bombarded with stimuli that influence us and these stimuli range on a spectrum from completely secular to completely spiritual. Unfortunately, the modern world is all too proficient at encouraging the material and discouraging the spiritual. Thus it's a challenge just to *recognize* one's spiritual self in today's world much less develop it!

## Stand Facing the Stove

[People have] two eyes
One only sees what moves in fleeting time
The other
What is eternal and divine.    *– The Book of Angelus Silesius*

Most people aren't focused on spiritual issues and don't make use of their spiritual eye. Like the newlywed who had never cooked much of anything before, you've got to look at the right things and in the right direction. The newlywed bought a book on cooking basics, opened to the first chapter and read, "Step One: Stand facing the stove!"

Likewise, as we awaken to that part of ourselves that has known God for all eternity, we begin to see that everyone has a relationship with God, whether they know it or not. But it takes a *choice* on the part of each individual to recognize one's spiritual sense and let it manifest in one's life.

So many people are focused on saving the world from its problems. Ironically, they are often blind to the one thing that might actually help bring about peace and healing – individual spiritual growth. Sure, it's difficult to change the world through the spiritual awareness and growth of individuals, but it's the *only* way we can move toward a world in which suffering is minimized.

Through individual spiritual development, we can foster love, compassion, altruism and peace throughout the world.

Individuals can change families, families can change communities, communities can change nations and nations can change the world! As Sant Rajinder Singh, president of the World Fellowship of Religions, says, "It is only when each individual has achieved inner peace that we will see lasting outer peace in the world."

By focusing on one's spirituality, an inner world opens in which one finds the key to an abundant, peaceful and joyful life. How do we begin this process? To start with our own spiritual awareness we must, paradoxically, look at the world.

# 2

# The Denial of God in the Modern World

Faith is the great mover of [humankind], and yet cannot be measured on the laboratory scales. — William Osler

Science without religion is lame; religion without science is blind. — Albert Einstein

Gallup polls regularly show that approximately 96 percent of Americans profess a belief in God and about 80 percent pray "regularly." This belief transcends socioeconomic status, age and gender, and these percentages have been virtually unchanged in polls over the past 50 years.

Interestingly, this faith exists in spite of the apprehension Americans feel about openly discussing their spirituality. It is also rather extraordinary that our spiritual pursuits have persisted in a world where science has been deified, where there is hostility to intangibles – that which cannot be empirically proven. Only after we are shown some "proof" of their existence, it seems, will spiritual truths be able to emerge in the modern world. This was very true for me.

## Opening the Heart through the Head

"Unless you see signs and wonders you will not believe."
 – Jesus of Nazareth to an official in Cana (Jn 4:48)

Today's "intelligentsia" tell us that if we are to be rational thinkers, we should not infer anything past the five senses, no matter what we "experience." In addition, the modern world relies on facts and data, and thus nothing can be truly believed and internalized unless it has been through the rigors of verification and the scientific method; even the nightly news shows us that we can barely believe what we see, much less what we don't see. Since the facts we receive daily on any topic often conflict, how can we give credence to something spiritual?

I believe that for many people in today's secular world, the heart must be opened *through the head.* That is, only after being given *reasons* to believe can they begin to open their heart and soul to their spiritual sense. Through reason, people can start *trusting their spiritual sense;* they can reconnect to the core knowledge of God that has been within them all along and initiate a process of personal growth.

How does this happen? With God's help, that's how. I believe the moment we "accept" and awaken to our spirituality – that is to our awareness of God – God begins to feed our heart and soul with the truth of God and God's plan for us. We start seeing our choices clearly and their effects on others, life begins to take on a different meaning, and we begin a slow but sure spiritual transformation into the person God intended us to be.

*Belief through Reason*

Any attempt made by scientists and theologians to validate or provide an empirical "reason" for spiritual tenets should, I believe, have an ultimate purpose; it should be used as a means to another end. Providing evidence of the workings of an omnipotent, benevolent deity as an end in itself (simply for the sake of proving God exists, as if that is what is most important about God) is pointless.

Furthermore, I have come across theologians and other learned spiritual scholars who consider belief through reason to be rather insulting to God. That is, they assert that it is offensive to God that we'll only "believe" in God if it can be proved God exists. We'll accept spirituality based upon some form of science but not based upon scripture (that which those involved in spiritual teachings view as their body of truth related from God). I understand this opinion and in principle I agree, but from a *practical* point of view I have seen that for many people "reason" can be the catalyst for spiritual growth.

I am willing to investigate the scientific bases for spiritual tenets only because I know the modern world's secular veil is so impenetrable that many people need some evidence for belief, a justification for a spiritual awareness. *Through reason they might have confidence in their spiritual sense, acknowledge their awareness of God, open their hearts and grow toward a deeper understanding of God and their spirituality.* Thus the end to the means of looking for empirical bases for belief is to be able to open the heart and reconnect to the eternal God.

Clearly I wish reasons were never necessary; it would be wonderful for people to reach a certain point in their lives when they mystically reconnect to God and nurture their spiritual growth. Unfortunately, this does not always happen. While one's true spiritual sense and belief in God has nothing to do with empiricism and reasoning, I have seen how the latter can assist in opening one's eyes to the former.

I *know* that scientific rationalism can be used to promote a spiritual search (in which scripture and the truth of God can then be made paramount) because that is what happened to *me*. I will never know exactly what happened that night in 1992 or during that pivotal point in my life. Nevertheless, I still wanted reasons to believe but only after my search began did I see that I really never needed them.

A good example of the use of reason is found in physicist Frank Tipler's book *The Physics of Immortality*. Tipler uses modern math and physics to show us God exists and says God is the Omega Point physicists have been talking about. Scientifically he shows that there will be a resurrection of the dead and life everlasting for all, defending his statements only with science. Nor does he use support from scripture, though it exists, for his conclusions. Because the world sees science as the truth teller, Tipler's scientific support for belief may be the catalyst for some people to explore and nurture their own spiritual sense, to begin a process of getting past the ever-present denial of the spiritual realm in the modern world.

## The Denial of God and Spirituality

> It is one of the commonest mistakes to consider that the limit of our power of perception is also the limit of all there is to perceive. — C.W. Leadbeater

I now understand that no one thing can hinder our spiritual growth like the large-scale *denial* of God in our lives. Don't get me wrong, I'm not suggesting we don't believe God exists; the vast majority of people do. I am saying, however, that we tend to live as though God doesn't exist.

Why is there such a denial? Large-scale denial exists because we have removed God from our daily lives. By deferring to the see-feel-touch world we have taken away God's place in what we call reality. If God is so important to most people, as polls continually tell us, then *why* do we relegate God to an existence outside of our real world – the one in which we live?

If we all have a spiritual sense, if most of us believe in God and if we accept that our spirituality is both real and important, then why do we, relatively speaking, ignore these things? Succinctly put, if they're so central to our existence, then why do we say we believe but act as if we don't? Let's face it. As a society, we're good talkers when it comes to our spiritual beliefs but our actions reflect a people devoid of spirituality.

*Conflicting Thoughts*

The intrapersonal driving mechanism for this denial is *cognitive dissonance* – the simultaneous existence within a person of cognitions (attitudes, thoughts, values and opinions) that do not fit together, usually on an issue of central importance. When we value one thing yet act or have thoughts motivating us to behave in a way inconsistent with that which we value, cognitive dissonance develops. For instance, a teenage girl raised to hold strict Roman Catholic values in high esteem may subsequently become pregnant and consider abortion. She will have a large degree of cognitive dissonance on this important issue.

Since cognitive dissonance is uncomfortable at best and mentally unhealthy at worst, one typically takes steps to reduce the discord. Often the path taken is the one requiring the least effort – sweeping the dissonance under the conscious mental rug, enabling denial to set in. Question: How do you reconcile the existence of God with a world in which human-made science reigns and innocent people suffer? Answer: Most people would say you just don't. Peace, tolerance and compassion? They only exist in a spiritual Fantasyland on Sunday morning not in our dog-eat-dog world. Miracles, premonitions and near-death experiences? Better not let anyone hear you talk about spiritual phenomena; they might think you're nuts.

What fascinates me about this denial is that if you ask people if they've ever had a spiritual experience, the majority will tell you they *have*. A good friend of mine who is a professor at a state university on the East Coast once described to me the following incident: After his father's funeral, he and his mother were grieving in their living room. The windows and doors were shut. Suddenly a piece of blue yarn lifted up off a table and floated across the room in front of them both. It got to the end of the room and fell to the floor. "It's just one of those things I can't explain," he told me. "But we both saw it with our own eyes." My friend is still a self-proclaimed agnostic.

In spite of what we feel and have experienced, we tend to defer to the world which has done everything it can to convince us that it alone shows us all of reality and holds the answers to the world's ultimate questions. Those things we hold as true stem from many areas—the most influential of them for most people being what the *world tells us is true*.

Since the descriptions of the world we encounter come from both *science* and *spiritual teachings*, let's look at the relation between these sources of information before examining the issues that tend to create cognitive dissonance, denial and obstacles to spiritual awareness and growth.

## The Myopia of Science

> Penetrating so many secrets, we cease to believe in the unknowable. But there it sits, nevertheless, calmly licking its chops.
> —H.L. Mencken

Know then, proud man, what a paradox you are to yourself.

Be humble, impotent reason! Be silent, feeble nature! Learn that man infinitely transcends man, hear from your master your true condition, which is unknown to you. Listen to God.                    —French mathematician Blaise Pascal

It is certainly possible that the conflict existing between science and spirituality is the most destructive influence on both the individual and society the world has seen in centuries. As someone who was vested in the scientific method, I had a belief in science alone that caused me to distrust and deny my spiritual self. This issue was particularly important to me the more I sought to understand God's role in the world.

Fueling this conflict is the fact that society as a whole has bought into the notion that science, with all its wonderful discoveries, advancements and new knowledge, is the only way to truly see the world, the only thing that really provides us with answers, direction and truth. Yet there are many fundamental problems with this concept, particularly in the natural and medical sciences.

For example, the late cosmologist Carl Sagan described science as a candle in a demon-haunted world. While science can shine light on and clarify issues clouded with myth and superstition, we must remember that we *created* the candle and it only illuminates what we have programmed it to, what we can understand. That is, there are other things present in the darkness our candle cannot yet illuminate. Also, since we developed the scientific method, humankind has given only itself ultimate control and has recognized no other force but the laws it can identify with its scientific tool and worldview. Finally, it is important to remember that our candle does, periodically, change in structure and has even occasionally led us astray.

Don't misinterpret what I'm saying here: science has been tremendously instrumental in providing a means of expanding our knowledge about the reality of our universe. Who would want to live in a world without it? Where would we be had we not created this tool, this rigid method for collecting data, formulating and testing hypotheses? Yet it has become clear to me that many researchers in science find little beyond a mechanistic universe which doesn't deviate from its orderly, predictable laws and patterns. This is a very naturalistic view, leaving no room for the spirit. Spiritual issues then become insignificant since they aren't seen to affect anything in the real world.

Likewise, the imperfect way science views truth and reality makes many wonder how much has science discovered of what there is to uncover? Our knowledge of the world increases every year due to the advancements reported in scientific literature, but how much more is there to ferret out? Have we found 99 percent of everything? Two percent? No one knows.

What we *do* know is that there is still a part of reality we do not yet have the tools to study. Phenomena we can only call miracles actually occur. Of course, just because we cannot measure them doesn't mean we should pretend they're not there. As anthropologist Margaret Mead said, "Because science expands one type of knowledge, it need not denigrate another. All great scientists have understood this."

## Outside The Blinders

> Assuredly, the real world is of a different temperament—
> more intricately built than physical science allows.
> —William James

Even in situations where the world clearly acts in an unpredictable and enigmatic manner, scientists—not knowing how to deal with something they don't understand and cannot see, feel or touch—simply say the mystery doesn't exist. This myopia in the medical sciences can be seen in how many physicians approach the spontaneous remissions of cancers. Spontaneous remission, for me, is a useless term used when a medical professional really wants to say, "This patient should have gotten worse. Instead, this patient got better, and I have no clue why."

However, we cannot overlook the obvious truth that something *did* indeed happen the patient. Here is the resultant irony: If there is one scientific philosophy both natural and medical scientists have been trained to rely on it is the cause-effect paradigm, known as determinism—a change occurred because something *caused* the change (the effect). Yet when it comes to effects in which an obvious, predictable cause—like the administration of a treatment or drug for which they are happy to take credit—cannot be seen or measured in their mechanistic universe, scientists have the habit of ignoring the effect.

Moreover, to humankind's most important spiritual questions science doesn't provide answers. As philosophy and religion scholar Huston Smith has said, "The worthful aspects of reality—its values, meaning and purpose—slip through the devices of science in the way that the sea slips through the nets of fishermen."

Of course, I do not blame science for its inability to provide answers to questions dealing with spiritual pursuits. In fact, science itself can be defined as "a socially organized instrument used to generate reliable knowledge about the natural world," not the supernatural world. Thus by virtue of the nature of spirituality, proving anything about it is likely to be impossible; since spirituality involves the transcendent, it may be inherently supra-empirical, unable to be scientifically examined.

How can we expect science, which uses human-made systems with limited power, to assess non-human-made systems with seemingly infinite power? (Remember, though, science itself is not naturalistic or atheistic; it's not looking in the direction of the spirit to begin with.) Even educated people today falsely believe that everything existing in nature will reveal itself so that we can experience it with our five senses or measure it with one of our instruments. How ridiculous!

St. Augustine, who noted that God could only be understood by the soul (not by the five senses) said, "Miracles happen, not in opposition to Nature, but in opposition to what we know of Nature." Edgar D. Mitchell, the Apollo 14 astronaut, explained, "The universe is a billion times more beautiful, abundant and malleable than humans ever dreamed it to be. We shape our 'reality' from the minuscule amount of information our sensory mechanisms gather and organize from experience into our 'map' of reality. . . . Whatever the nature of the ultimate reality, humans can only consciously discern it through the lens of our sensors and as shaped by belief. Thus far in human history we have been perceiving the universe and ourselves in a very limiting fashion."

It is important to remember that the rigidity of the scientific method mandates scientists to use *blinders* and to focus solely in one direction. However necessary and useful this might be, we must also accept that when we wear blinders, we can miss much that is truly there – outside the blinders and on the periphery. We must all be careful to ensure that the scientific experiment itself does not become the final arbitrator of truth and reality. We must make certain that we do not make a God of the scientific method and a religion of science.

## Spirituality as Trivial

Is our generation so proud, so self-centered, so critical of everything that cannot be measured by the micrometers and gauges of the natural world, so called, that it has become of the earth earthly, and has lost all capacity to grasp and appropriate the no less 'natural' realities in the realm of the spirit?  – James Richard Joy

Along with the elevation of science as truth-teller, we have trivialized the importance of spirituality. During my search and journey of spiritual awareness and truth, finding three very pertinent and consequential issues in this relegation of spirituality and God to second fiddle was a welcome revelation.

First, the separation of science from spirituality has only occurred in the relatively recent past. Second, in the vast majority of cases, the groundbreaking researchers involved were strong spiritual persons–believers themselves who did *not* differentiate scientific from spiritual pursuits. Third, until recently scholars of science and spiritual teachings have attempted to work together to form models of the universe that satisfied *both* bodies of knowledge. What follows is a very brief history of science and thought illustrating these points.

Plato, the great Athenian philosopher of the fourth century BC, probably first discussed the existence of the ultimate source of goodness–though it is still debated whether he was monotheistic–from a rational or "scientific" standpoint. Specifically, he described the *cosmological* argument for the existence of a God: since there is a creation, so there must be a creator. According to Plato, some first cause must have started it all. Consistent with this, he argued that as there are "contingent" beings (humans) there must be a "necessary" being to explain the existence of contingent beings. This creator and necessary being, this absolute reality was, he believed, the single supreme idea of good–God.

Aristotle, Plato's student who later developed the basis for Western thought, believed the question of God and spirituality to be much more valuable than anything involving matter. Aristotle suggested we can come to know God by *reason,* not solely by faith and put the proofs of God into strictly scientific form. God, referred to as the "unmoved mover," was the ultimate source of knowledge, order and perfection in the universe.

## Three Upheavals

From Plato and Aristotle's time to the present there have been three great scientific revolutions threatening the thought of the day. First, in the 12th and 13th centuries, Aristotelian philosophy was rediscovered, chiefly by friar Thomas Aquinas. A good scientist and philosopher, Aquinas saw his inquiries into the nature of the world as religious quests. During this period, called "late antiquity," science and philosophy were tied to religion and scientific study; thus philosophical questions were essentially religious questions. Aquinas took Aristotelian physics and used it to prove the existence of God. God brought science and theology together in a unique manner where science's first priority was to serve spirituality. The synthesis that resulted – Aquinas's *Summae* – consolidated the two bodies of thought. Neither science nor theology saw it as perfect, but it was at least acceptable.

The second great upheaval occurred during the scientific revolution of the 16th and 17th centuries. Polish astronomer and priest Nicholas Copernicus and German astronomer Johannes Kepler, who believed God was somehow mystically involved in the mathematical computations of the solar system, both saw their cosmology as serving God. In 1524 Copernicus overturned the Roman Catholic church's view of the Earth as center of universe through his calculations. In the early 17th century Italian astronomer Galileo Galilei made it possible to confirm the Copernican view with his telescope. Despite being under house arrest until the end of his life for his assertions, Galileo remained a faithful Roman Catholic.

Also in the 17th century, French mathematician and philosopher René Descartes used reason and logic from mathematics to prove the existence of God. He wrote that his arguments demonstrating the existence of God, "were drawn up in geometrical fashion." Descartes believed that God was every bit as certain as a mathematical formula and used mathematical terms as analogies to communicate his argument to others. For example, Descartes would explain, "that God exists is as clear as the fact that a triangle has three sides." Just as there can be no three-sided square by definition – it contradicts itself – a person denying the existence of God is contradictory – since, by definition, that which was created had a Creator.

Descartes, the originator of analytical geometry, held a view that separated mind and matter and he expounded upon the growing rationalistic and naturalistic thinking of the 17th century. Likewise, Descartes believed he was describing none other than God's laws and considered himself a good Catholic.

English physicist Sir Isaac Newton provided the mathematical laws that supported Descartes' (the "Cartesian") view. He explained that the orderliness of the universe can be predicted mathematically since the universe had deterministic, causal principles. Newtonian physics described the classical laws of matter and energy and gave us the scientific basis for a mechanistic view of universe – a universe based on "cause-effect" relations.

This Newtonian model affected all other sciences and in spite of philosopher David Hume's subsequent and persuasive argument that cause-effect relations (determinism) were based upon experiences and not reason, the Newtonian model became the foundation for answering scientific questions. It is also noteworthy that Newton had strong religious convictions. He saw his work as describing a worldview where God imposes divine laws and is a cosmic Designer who works through them. Newton once wrote that nothing could "rejoice" him more than if his science could be used to prove the existence of God.

It should be of no surprise that even after the second upheaval in scientific thought, scholars from science and spirituality proposed acceptable consolidations of their views, giving birth to Deism and "Rational Christianity" where some evidence of Design and God were still seen as necessary. God, they felt, set these laws in motion as one would wind a watch, yet remained uninvolved at a distance. Newton, a devout Christian, detailed a harmony of scientific and spiritual truths.

The third great scientific upheaval began in the late 18th century. According to many post-Newton scientists who interpreted his work differently than did Newton and his contemporaries, miracles were impossible because they operated outside of reason and the orderly, mechanistic manner in which the universe ran. Thus God could not be proved and humanity, they felt, should be considered to be the center of the universe.

Fueling this new thinking was Charles Darwin's *Origin of Species* (1859) and Freud's theories of the mind—both described a world in which God was neither important nor needed. More and more, nature was seen as placed under human control and those who looked to spiritual wisdom instead of science for answers were regarded as naïve. Following this tumult, however, there was no attempt at consolidation. There was no compromise, no correction. Thus the scientific establishment began its reign while many within it believed the future of humankind was independent of God.

*Separate Ways*

Slowly God became increasingly irrelevant in the modern empirical world. Spurred on by Darwinism, Modernist thinkers began elevating scientific rationalism as the only true source of knowledge—for society in general as well as for physical phenomena. As science has achieved much in the past 200 years through the scientific method, the chasm between science and spirituality has only gotten wider (though the split was only

36                                             Reasons to Believe

meant to separate religious dogma from science). During this same period, to the degree that spirituality has become increasingly disconnected from the "truth-teller" science, it has also been seen as disconnected from empirical "knowledge."

The scientific metamorphosis through Darwin began the trivialization of God and spirituality in general. The technological advances of the past two centuries, riding on the waves of naturalism (the belief that the universe can be understood without including God) and science, have nearly finished them off. Despite the vast majority of scientists noting, if not working for, spiritual pursuits, God gradually became an also-ran.

To worsen matters, in order to keep religion somewhat respectable in a new scientific age, many theologians during this same period abandoned any real objective, empirical content within religion and redefined it as symbolic. In an obvious attempt to reduce the discord between new scientific understanding and religious thought, many theologians unwittingly created a modern theology that has become even more irrelevant to science with the result that religion and science are often seen as mutually exclusive and completely disconnected.

Hindering any consolidation, contemporary scientists often reject their spiritual selves in favor of science as the ultimate truth-finder. Additionally, a large degree of their time and self-worth is vested in empiricism; it is what made them important and valuable. World-renowned scientist George Smoot received much criticism when, describing a recent monumental discovery in physics that relates to the beginning of the universe, he said, "If you're religious, it's like looking at God." He went on to explain, "Most criticism came from scientists who find the idea threatening because it's an unresolved issue personally. To get into science, a lot of scientists may have rejected religion initially but then later never went back and got comfortable with that rejection."

## Harmony

> Everyone who is seriously involved in the pursuit of science becomes convinced that a Spirit is manifest in the Laws of the Universe. . . .  —Albert Einstein

> The equations of physics have in them incredible simplicity, elegance and beauty. That in itself is sufficient to prove to me that there must be a God who is responsible for these laws and responsible for the universe.  —Paul Davies

Ironically I discovered that over the past few decades, spiritual teachings and scripture have garnered *more*, not less, support from science. Likewise, many scientists no longer see the need to remain locked in their empiricism, now believing they have separated themselves too far and for too long from truth that can only be understood spiritually. In fact, physician and researcher Melvin Morse describes a "secret club" of spiritually-oriented doctors and scientists who are emerging, having become less fearful of criticism from their scientific colleagues.

Recent evidence in various scientific fields has experts on both sides questioning whether the pendulum has swung too far towards the empirical—perhaps there should be an effort to balance and re-center. This movement toward the spirit is slow but sure. Walter Bradley of Texas A&M explains that "scientific understanding and the attitudes of many modern scientists have moved strongly toward belief in an intelligent creator as a result of the scientific discoveries of the past 35 years."

Every one of us should embrace and support science and all its achievements. Science continues to provide us with ways to enhance the lives of all people. However, even considering the advancements the various bodies of scientific knowledge have endowed the world with this century, we must ensure that the empirical is not presented at the expense of the spiritual.

I now see that a great deal of harmony exists between scientific and spiritual tenets, though zealousness and downright arrogance often keeps those inside these fields from seeing it clearly. Often scientists and theologians are talking about the same things, but use different sources of information and different methods to discuss them.

*A Matter of Necessity*

Though "reasons to believe" in today's world can *often* be effective in awakening one's spirituality, it is not my opinion that one *needs* to affirm one's spiritual self through "proof" or consistency with science. Neither is it of particular interest to most scientists for their theories to be supported by spiritual tenets. However, it is destructive both personally and socially to make every effort, as we have, to live as if science and spirituality were mutually exclusive, especially when harmony is becoming more and more obvious.

Can these two real sources of knowledge coexist peacefully? I feel that they *must*. Now more than ever we have very serious social problems, deadly infectious diseases and bioethical dilemmas, such as genetic engineering and cloning, and need the best of both worlds side-by-side if we are to resolve them.

Now that we've looked at the relation between science and spirituality, I'd like to return to how this unfortunate parting of the ways has contributed to the widespread removal of God and spiritual issues from both our social and personal lives (each of the latter affecting the other), and how the resulting disharmony has manifested itself to the detriment of our being. Thus we will look at the various factors creating the cognitive dissonance which results in the large-scale personal and social denial of God and our spiritual sense—the main roadblock to spiritual awareness and growth in the modern world.

# 3

# In the Beginning

The surest path to knowing God is through the study of science and for that reason God started the Bible with a description of the creation.
— Medieval philosopher Moses Maimonides

If the conflict existing between science and spirituality is, at the least, a very destructive influence on both the individual and society today, then clearly the *origin and creation of the universe and life* (including humankind) may be the single largest *issue* in this conflict. The "creation" problem manifests as the most obvious roadblock to a foundation of harmony between science and spirituality, pitting one body of knowledge and "truth" against the other while, at the same time, fostering cognitive dissonance and destructive spiritual denial.

I discovered early in my search that this dilemma was, without doubt, the primary issue causing my inner conflict. I felt that if science – in which I was immersed most of my time – had disproved spiritual tenets on this most fundamental matter, then there would eventually be a *limit* to how much credence I could give to my spiritual sense, no matter how great the intensity of my feelings or beliefs. I had to understand this issue, and though I initially assumed that origin and creation were exclusively in the domain of science, I nonetheless felt called to explore it.

Parenthetically, I don't think I'm alone here. In my talking with many secular groups, the "creation problem" comes up frequently as a source of their dissonance and spiritual denial. I am certain many people relegate a great deal of their spirituality to "myth" status when encountering confusion about the most fundamental issue of what created the universe and life. If God was a "no show" in creation, it's doubtful that God's a big part of our lives now, the thinking goes. If we didn't need God then, surely we can get by without God now. If the creation account is just a nice story, what other aspects of scripture can we discount? Not only do I believe the creation problem to be of absolute and vital importance to me, but its reconciliation can be a unifying force for society in general.

This seemingly irreconcilable dilemma of creation comes from answers to two important questions: First, how was the "universe" (a term I will use to mean all matter between and within all galaxies, often called "cosmos") formed? Second, how were life and humankind created? I'll look at these questions using information from both the most recent scientific literature and longstanding spiritual literature – scripture.

Scientific literature and scripture have two very different accounts for the creation of the universe and life – namely (a) a divinely created universe and life being formed in six days and (b) random acts of nature forming the universe and life over the course of 15 billion years. These two explanations appear at the outset to be completely irreconcilable.

This issue has contributed greatly to the continued rift and general separation of thought between these two bodies. Since the past 200 years have disconnected science and spirituality and hindered any consolidation between them, and since the reign of science is based upon what it can provide as evidence, we, as a scientifically advanced society, have naturally accepted a creation account void of divine intervention; after all, there are no "God fossils." So God and spirituality have gone the way of the Easter Bunny and Santa Claus – childhood stories that worked for a while but then we all have to grow up sometime and see the world as it really is, right?

That's what I thought, until I came across Gerald Schroeder's pivotal book, *Genesis and the Big Bang.* Through the use of science and its findings, Schroeder, formerly a physicist at the Massachusetts Institute of Technology, showed how the established scientific truths we have always embraced about the origin of the universe and humankind are also harmonious with creation as described in scripture. Though many scientists have attempted to explain the harmony they have seen between matter and spirit, for me none have done it in such a clever, astute manner, and with such consequential, paramount questions. After in-depth research into Schroeder's thesis, I found his general theory to be fascinating, brilliant and revolutionary. At worst, Schroeder's scientific principles – themselves solid and well-accepted – may only be slightly misapplied. At best, he has illuminated a spiritual pathway for people in the modern world to follow, a road on which they can live as fully spiritual beings.

I have refined Schroeder's argument to one I believe to be more accurate in its application to scripture. However, the lion's share of my version I owe to him (and a few other scientists). More importantly, my subsequent spiritual awakening, resulting from seeing the modern world through both secular *and* spiritual eyes, I also owe to him.

Here, then, is a genuine way scientists and spiritual scholars can talk about the beginnings of the universe and evolution intelligently without denigrating each other or resorting to preposterous rationalizations. It is a new paradigm for seeing the development of the universe and humankind that can be appreciated from either the scientific or scriptural vantage point. Moreover, it is a way we can begin to break down the secular walls within which we live and can validate our spiritual sense, reconnecting ourselves to a relationship with the eternal God.

## A Problem of Time

Scripture indicates that it took six days to create the universe, life and humankind. The scriptural scholar who calculates the ages of all the generations of people recorded in the Bible since the appearance of Adam finds that the universe and humankind are certainly no more than 10,000 years old.

I say here unequivocally that this idea had no basis in our knowledge of the physical universe. Scientific evidence puts the age of the universe at 15 billion years with fossil records of human-like beings roughly up to two million years old (the recently discovered fossilized skulls in Java are human-like). These fossils absolutely do exist; scriptural scholars must accept them as true so as not to be hypocritical when accusing scientists of wearing blinders.

The simplest forms of life (prokaryotic bacteria and blue-green algae exposed in early sedimentary rock in Africa and Australia) originated a few hundred million years after the Earth's crust cooled and solidified and have been dated – at approximately 3.5 billion years old by the very reliable methods of geochronology using decaying Uranium and end-product Lead isotope rations, or Potassium-40/Argon decay. How do you reconcile that the universe is roughly 15 billion years old, the Earth about 4.5 billion years old and evidence of life beginning approximately 3.5 billion years ago with a six day creation? That was my question, too.

Obviously, when it comes to the creation of the universe and life, *time* is the problem – the seemingly impermeable wall between "truthseekers" on both sides. It would appear that there is no place for common ground – 15 billion years and six days don't come close. To be sure, it's not just a matter of perception – as W.C. Fields once explained, "One night I spent a week in Philadelphia."

So scriptural scholars who adhere to the belief that the universe with all its life was created in six Earthly days and refuse to acknowledge what paleontologists have physical evidence of, realize they must do something to account for this tremendous difference. Rationalizations such as the following are sophomoric at best or blatantly inconsistent with both science *and* scripture at worst:

- God put very old fossils of life there to test our faith;
- Satan put these fossils there to deceive us;
- Radioactive isotope dating is wrong because the decay patterns of paleontological matter have changed as a result of Noah's flood. (NB: There is no known way to modify half-lives of radioactive isotopes);
- Allocating each day about 2.5 billion years. (NB: Scripture does clearly say there was morning and evening, one day.)

Yet I have said that I will show how harmony can be attained simply if scientists and spiritualists are open to each other and willing to see clearly. Is this possible? Yes.

You see *both* are correct; they are describing the exact same thing. It *did* take six days *and* 15 billion years, simultaneously, starting at the same instant and finishing at the same instant. I know you've got to see this to believe it. First, let me clarify.

When you look at how scientific literature and scripture relate to each other in their accounts of the "beginning" it is interesting to note that everything occurring after the creation of the universe, life and humankind is *temporally consistent*. Thus everything *after* the creation of Adam is both well-established by and harmonious with science and scripture. In my research, I realized this was well accepted by scientists and theologians alike, even to my own surprise as I (a) am far from a scriptural literalist, and (b) understand that the Bible was not written to be a historical document (though many scholars now regard the Old Testament as an actual "history of a people").

For example, the invention of forged brass tools is related in scripture as having happened at a particular point in time, subsequently confirmed by science. The Bible says Tubal-Cain, son of Lamech, was responsible for developing brass (Gn 4:22). When we calculate scriptural ages, we see the time that Tubal-Cain invented forging was about 1,350 years after the appearance of the man called Adam, or roughly 4,400 years before the present. Archaeologically, the appearance of early brass tools is seen at roughly 2400 BC, about 4,400 years ago. In science and history we call the time of Tubal-Cain the early Bronze Age.

In 1853 Henry Rawlinson's excavations at Borsippa near Babylon in southern Mesopotamia unearthed commemorative cylinders that recorded how Nebuchadnezzar, king of Babylon, rebuilt and repaired the temple there in the early sixth century BC. In the 1860s, Charles Warren excavated the underground water channel that Hezekiah constructed beneath Jerusalem (2

Kg 20:20). Also, the scriptural account of Joshua's conquest of Canaan, his burning of the city of Hazor and the subsequent rebuilding of Hazor by Solomon 300 years later corroborate perfectly the findings of scientists during the recent excavation of Hazor. Researchers discovered the charred ruins of a burned city and above this was built a new city, complete with Solomon's uniquely shaped gates and horse stables.

The point I'm making is that what functionally may be the *single most divisive issue* between science and spirituality in the modern world comes down to what happens in just *the very first part of Genesis*. For many, as it was for me, this is the only major divisive issue causing a science-spirit conflict, cognitive dissonance and denial, and relegating the Genesis account and much of one's spirituality to myth. So, how can I say both are right? How do I reconcile two very different accounts of the beginning of the universe and life? With a little help from a genius.

Hang on, it's not too difficult to grasp.

### It Took an Einstein

In 1900 few would have thought science would see beyond three dimensional space and time. Beyond length, height and width what else could there be? Then in 1905 Albert Einstein published a series of papers undermining classical Newtonian physics and forever changing the way physicists see the world. Einstein argued that space was not three-dimensional and time was not a separate linear entity. Time was seen as intertwined with space making a fourth dimension of space-time which completely altered our view of the passage of time and had tremendous implications for the Biblical creation account.

*Special theory of relativity*

Let's back up. As you know, we see objects because light illuminates them. Immediately before Einstein's 1905 papers, scientist Max Planck proposed his quantum theory for light which states that light's elementary particles (which he called "quanta" and Einstein later called "photons") transcend the dimensions of space and time. Einstein added to this concept of light as unique when he discovered that the speed of light was constant, though other matter did not behave this way.

Specifically, Einstein determined that photons move at a speed roughly 300,000 KM per sec (or more simply, 300 million meters per sec – a kilometer is a thousand meters) and have mass while in motion but no mass when stopped. Einstein later described this as $E = mc^2$, where the energy (E) of a photon equals it mass (m) while in motion times the speed of light squared ($c^2$). Thus mass, Einstein argued, is nothing but a form of energy; energy and mass are essentially one in the photon.

In addition, when the velocity of an object changes, its mass changes. So Einstein took Planck's ideas on light "quanta" transcending space and time, added his own observations of light energy, mass and velocity, and related them both to the 300-year-old concepts of Galileo, who explained that all the laws of nature are the same in all systems having smooth, uniform motion ("inertial reference frames"). The result of these phenomena, Einstein predicted, is that strange things will happen not necessarily within reference frames but *across* reference frames (because the motion of non-light matter is not constant). In essence, he claimed the velocity of light – 300 million meters per second – is *constant* not only when everything is moving at the same speed (within reference frames), but also when they're not (across reference frames)!

*Crossing Reference Frames and Crazy Space-Time.* If I've confused you, here's a hypothetical example of what Einstein said: You're piloting a plane miles away from an airport control tower. Your plane loses power, you land safely so the air traffic controller sends you an emergency repair plane traveling at 300 mph. You and the controller in the tower are motionless (in the same reference frame) and both see the plane traveling at 300 mph—toward you and away from him.

Suddenly, you get your plane started and decide to head back to the airport in the same line of flight as the repair plane. You fly toward it at 100 mph. The speed of the repair plane relative to you is 400 mph (300 mph + 100 mph), and the speed of the repair plane relative to the controller in the tower is still 300 mph, right? Right. This is what you would expect; the controller sees the speed differently than you do because you're not in the same reference frame (you're moving; the control tower is motionless). Everything is fine, velocity is simply additive for you.

The next day the exact same thing happens to your plane, but this time instead of sending a repair plane, the control tower flashes you a *light* signal which, of course, travels to you at the speed of light—300 million meters/sec. Again you and the controller are both in the same reference frame (motionless) and both see the flash moving at the speed of light—toward you and away from him. Once again your plane regains power and you take off in the direction of the light being flashed to you. Remember, as before, we're dealing with two different reference frames—one for you and one for the controller.

What do you see? Light approaching you at 300 million meters/sec plus 100 mph? No! You *still* see the light approaching you at only 300 million meters/sec even though you're adding your speed to the speed of the light! (Of course, the controller in the tower sees the light moving away from his stationary position at 300 million meters/sec.)

Why does this happen? No one really knows; it's frustrating and mind-boggling. How can you *both* measure the same speed for the light when one is moving toward it and one is standing still? It's baffling but true! The point here is that light, *regardless* of the velocity of the observer to the light source (that is, even across reference frames) is *always* 300 million meters/sec. So the speed of light–the way we see things–is an absolute constant, even though the motion of all other matter is *not constant* but relative.

Another analogy might help: When we see a shadow, we're observing the image of a three-dimensional person on a two-dimensional object. How your shadow appears to you depends upon the positioning of that two-dimensional object (a wall, floor, screen, etc.). The concept of space-time is similar. With space-time we're measuring a fourth dimension in three-dimensional space; how it appears depends on the frame of reference of the three-dimensional person. We cannot experience the space-time dimension with our senses, we can only experience its three-dimensional images.

What's the conclusion? It is simply that when we travel across reference frames–from a frame that is in motion to a stationary one–then space-time gets very interesting. People actually see things happening in different temporal orders depending on their velocity relative to that which is observed. But what does all this have to do with spirituality and the occurrences in early Genesis? Keep reading; you'll see, as I did.

*Personal Clocks and Time Dilation.* Because of this and $E = mc^2$, Einstein explained that all observers carry around their own personal scale of time, not necessarily agreeing with anyone else's. In your own reference frame, time is never distorted, but compared to other observers moving differently, your time can be different than their time.

Likewise, Einstein demonstrated that time is elastic and can be stretched or modified by motion, a concept known as "time dilation." That is, time will get longer as *velocity*, relative to the observer, increases. Thus, if a space ship is moving away from you at 90 percent speed of light you will see those in the ship doing everything in slow motion. Even clocks will slow down. Einstein said, "No two events that are separated in space can be regarded as having happened at exactly the same moment."

To summarize, dimensions in space and the passage of time are *relative* to the relationship between the observer and the observed. Though this concept is at odds with our usual see-hear-touch, linear-time way of looking at the world, it is factual!

*General relativity*

In 1916, Einstein factored in another force that can influence the motion of objects—gravity. He considered the inclusion of gravity into the mix to be a "generalization" of his theory of relativity. In his general theory, Einstein predicted that gravity can also cause time dilation since it also influenced the *motion* of objects. Since gravity is related to mass and can be different in various parts of the universe (depending on the distribution of matter in the universe), it must also affect the perception of space-time.

By factoring in gravity, Einstein concluded that space-time should curve, that it would more likely be warped than flat. Gravity was described not as a force, but as a distortion of space-time produced by both matter and energy. Of course, space will curve to different degrees and time will flow at different rates in different parts of the universe (again, depending on the distribution of matter).

The notion of time dilation can be difficult to grasp. However, for time dilation to occur, we must be dealing with speeds at or near the speed of light, and we don't normally encounter these speeds. They do, though, occur in cosmology and physics. Yet keep in mind that we can only experience differences in the passage of time when comparing things *across* two reference frames, and even then we'll notice it only when vastly different gravitational forces and/or tremendous velocities exist.

*What It All Means*

Special and general relativity show us that space and time are unified in a fourth dimension and are relative, not absolute. The world of the very big going very fast means space-time is bendable! Taken together, and more pertinent to us, the principle of relativity and the constancy of light across reference frames brings us to the true phenomenon of time dilation.

Although it was revolutionary when presented, it is fair to say that Einstein's theory of relativity is now the Law of Relativity since so much of it has been shown to be true. During the solar eclipse on May 29, 1919, Arthur Eddington organized a famous test of general relativity which corroborated Einstein's prediction that light would bend as it passed near the Sun (demonstrating the curvature of space-time as a function of gravity). Additionally, when the Hubble telescope recently captured images of VirgoM87, it found a spiral disk rotating at about 1.2 million miles per hour around a center point—conclusive proof of Einstein's general theory of relativity (light can be trapped by a gravity field that's strong enough).

Even time dilation at velocities below the speed of light has been measured. Hafele and Keating at Washington University and the US Naval Observatory confirmed both special *and* general relativity by sending four cesium-beam clocks around the world on commercial aircraft and then comparing them to stationary clocks on the ground. To test for special relativity, they found that on the eastward flights, the flying clocks lost time relative to the clocks on the ground (since the Earth rotates from west to east) while on westward flights the flying clocks gained time. In their test for general relativity, Hafele and Keating had assumed that since gravity decreases as an object moves farther from the Earth's surface, a change in time should occur. In fact, the exact difference in time matched what was calculated from motion and gravity!

Einstein opened up a whole new world to the scientist and spiritual scholar alike, one that allows harmony to exist between their views. As I saw and as I'll show you in a moment, not only does $E=mc^2$ mean that space-time is bendable and different across reference frames, it also means that, depending on the vantage point of the observer, six days *does* equal 15 billion years! As scientist Paul Pearsall has written, "Albert Einstein's theory of relativity helps us begin to understand that time is not fixed in a one-way system; that time is a matter of the timekeeper and not the clock."

### A Changing of the Timekeeper

> . . . one day is with the Lord as a thousand years, and a
> thousand years as one day. —2 Peter 3:8

> For a thousand years in thy sight are but as yesterday when
> it is past, and as a watch in the night. —Psalm 90:4

Now I know what you're thinking. You can see this easy and convenient solution coming from a mile away, right? Any time two events are temporally inconsistent, just invoke relativity and make them consistent. *No,* that's not the case at all. Certainly, anyone investigating the effects of space-time relativity on an event must be able to show the *likelihood that reference frames—timekeepers—were different.* It must be clear that either scientific literature or scripture describes the two references frames as being dissimilar. Does either one describe a difference in the reference frames? Yes, scripture does.

The scriptural verses cited above metaphorically claim that time is a completely different dimension for the creator. Remember, to many people scripture is the essence of spiritual wisdom, the truth-teller in spiritual teachings and the inspired message of God. Interestingly, there is a place in early scripture, namely the second chapter of Genesis, *which is precisely the point where time moves from being inconsistent to consistent,* where a different reference frame is discussed.

Here are three points to consider. First, whether we distill the message of scripture or the read scripture literally, it is clear that God didn't make the heavens and Earth in one instant; there was a process of making ("For in six days the Lord made heaven and earth," [Ex 20:11]).

Second, the question then arises, "*Could* there have been a common clock between the vantage point described in the process of creation in the first chapters of Genesis and any vantage point on Earth?" The answer clearly is no! The creation description in early Genesis *must* have been described from a completely different reference frame for the following reason: We know that the process of creation required a mixing of matter from all over the universe. Indeed, even *we* are made up of cosmic debris from many parts of the universe.

Since the creation began time itself, which was dependent upon differences in gravitational forces, motions and masses—making time a very local issue for every planet—then *whose reference frame could possibly have been used to describe it all?* Likewise, since many clocks started at the Big Bang, each of which was different, but locally correct (in its reference frame), in what way could any time be described such that it would be locally correct everywhere?

As an analogy, if every room in the building you're now in had a different, but room-correct time and rate of time passage, how would you go about telling someone how much time passed in the creation of the building and every room? The answer is that you couldn't, *unless* you use a universal, outside-of-the-building time frame to describe the creation from a point exterior to everyone's room.

Therefore, the final point to understand here is that in the case of the creation of the universe the only reference frame that could make sense – the one that is common to all – is *the reference frame that encompasses the entirety of the universe, God's reference frame.* What else could one expect? What could the reference frame of the creator of every part of the universe have been? It seems only reasonable that the description of the creation and the events that immediately follow it in the beginning of Genesis *had* to include the totality of everything that was, all of creation.

*God and Time.* What is God's relationship to time, anyway? While that is still a mystery, our predecessors as well as present-day scientists talk about God's involvement in space-time and its "beginning" in much the same way. Einstein's general theory of relativity predicts *space-time began* when the entire universe exploded from an infinitely small and concentrated point at the Big Bang.

It is also worth noting that even famed physicist Stephen Hawking, who is certainly not motivated to provide evidence of spiritual wisdom, has shown his "no boundary" cosmology, where *time in itself becomes part of what is created,* to be remarkably similar to Einstein's theory. Moreover, Einstein's relativity and Hawking's no-boundary cosmology in part explain and are consistent with (a) St. Basil's fourth century writings which said that God's commands, "Let there be," took place timelessly but gave rise to orderly sequences in the world of space and time, and (b) St. Augustine's fifth century view, the "Ex Nihilo" (out of nothing) doctrine of creation, which addressed how a temporal universe was created by a *timeless deity*.

According to these scientists and early theologians, there was no "before" the Big Bang. They describe a model of the universe where time gradually emerges with it, showing how it is more likely that God created the universe *with* time rather than *in* time. Even astrophysicist Hugh Ross has said:

> If time's beginning is concurrent with the beginning of the universe, as the space-time theorem says, then the cause of the universe must be some entity operating in a time dimension completely independent of and preëxistent to the time dimension of the cosmos. . . . [This conclusion] tells us that the creator is transcendent, operating beyond the dimensional limits of the universe.

## Possible Applications

*Your Numbered Days*

It is fascinating that Einstein's theory of relativity opens up the possibility that in the 16th century John Calvin grasped hold of a tiny bit of truth–albeit, I believe, misunderstood even by him–when he outlined his highly unpopular *Doctrine of Predestination* (saying all sinners are condemned before they're born, but through mercy, God has already chosen some of them to be redeemed). Calvin, most scholars would argue and I would agree, was wrong in his insistence that God chose those certain souls to be redeemed prior to their actions and expressions of free will on Earth.

Yet Einstein showed us that past, present and future have already occurred *depending upon a person's reference frame*. Perhaps, as God dwells outside all reference frames (though God's eternal, all-encompassing vantage point contains the totality of all parts of the universe and their reference frames), God sees all future events in creation prior to their occurrence; maybe, as God sees all time from a vantage point external to it, God already knows who on Earth will be redeemed and who will not.

Thus, we encounter the notion that the book may have already been written, just not yet read – at least not here in our reference frame. In this small way, we may see some semblance of accuracy with one aspect of Calvin's doctrine. In the Psalms King David sings to the Lord: "Your eyes beheld my unformed substance. In your book were written all the days that were formed for me, when none of them as yet existed" (139:16).

*Future Sight*

Even from a scientific standard, we have seen clear evidence of the phenomenon of "future sight," where some people are able to foresee events to come – not predict, actually see them occur in explicit detail. Unfortunately, genuine cases of future sight often become occluded by charlatans posing as psychics or fortune-tellers. Such fraud prevents many from accepting those with this rare God-given ability. Perhaps future sight, and in essence prophecy, is a gift stemming from the ability for a brief time to tap into a vantage point where Earth's past, present and future can be seen.

## God's Description

Without a doubt, the reference frame and passage of time in the scriptural description of the creation would have to have been markedly different than whatever would have been described from a local vantage point on Earth. As Schroeder wrote: "When the Bible describes the day-by-day development of our universe in the six days following the creation, it is truly referring to six 24-hour days. But the reference frame by which those days were measured was one which contained the total universe." Thus creation lasted 15 billion years on Earth *and* six universal days in the reference frame of God – both beginning and ending at exactly the same time.

## The Genesis Break

Having explained the necessity for the unique recording of time in the scriptural "creation" account, I'm back to identifying the scriptural support for a point where time between spiritual tenets and science moves from being inconsistent to consistent, where local time takes over. This point occurs very clearly in the second chapter of Genesis.

When examining early Genesis, most people are surprised to find *two* creation accounts. You may recall that immediately after the first and more popular account of the creation (the "In the beginning" account), which ends with the description of the seventh day (Gn 2:3), there is an interesting verse – one that doesn't seem to fit – "These are the generations of the heavens and of the earth when they were created, *in the day* that the Lord God made the earth and the heavens" (Gn 2:4).

Then the second creation account begins. It's as if beginning at Genesis 2:5, scripture reverses itself and goes about explaining the creation from a *completely different orientation and vantage point, one more relative to humankind;* it deals much more personally with the creation of humankind, its environment and relationship with God. In fact, virtually nothing about the writing and orientation in the second creation account is similar to the "In the beginning" account.

## "In the Day"

> These are the generations of the heavens and of the earth
> when they were created, *in the day* that the Lord God made
> the earth and the heavens.               −Genesis 2:4

Besides the fact that Genesis 2:4 is the point in scripture after which the "personal," humankind-oriented creation is described, something else very interesting occurs at this verse, making the temporal break more clear. This unusual use of word "day" in the second part of the verse ("in the day that the Lord God made the earth and the heavens") certainly doesn't make sense if treated as a continuation from the first account. When we look at the original Hebrew, we find that translations of the Torah describe the phrase "in the day" as the Hebrew idiom for "at the time when."

Moreover, in standard use, the word "day" has been used either to mean (a) one single morning-to-night day, as when God separated light from darkness on the first day, or (b) a general period of time or era. Clearly, the former was not the intended use of "day" in that verse because the creation account had already indicated that it took six days, not one, to form the heavens and the earth. Thus, the Genesis 2:4 use of the word "day," for "general time when," was what was being conveyed.

Why else would this term be used other than to signify a change in the "clock"? It obviously would not be used if the reference frames and recordings of time were going to remain the same. This sentence, I believe, was well calculated by the author of Genesis to communicate that a completely different reference frame and recording of time was to begin in contrast to the first creation account when time was expressed as that occurring within the entire universe, not just Earth.

Most scholars look past the second creation account which

follows Genesis 2:4, though all would agree it contains a decidedly new orientation to humans, one that is unique – more personal and close. However, some such as renowned Biblical scholar Richard Friedman at the University of San Diego, see Genesis 2:4 as a significant new beginning which is as important as "In the beginning." In fact, Friedman's newest book, *The Hidden Book in the Bible*, has one chapter appropriately entitled "In the Day," where Friedman describes Genesis 2:4 as the point at which God's relationship to humans began anew.

Thus, following Genesis 2:4, humankind began a new, intimate and special relationship with God and the Earth's clock then became the best timekeeper to record ensuing events. From that point on, there is complete corroboration between scripture and science.

Whether you look at early Genesis to extract the message conveyed, as do I, or rely on its literal interpretation, it is unequivocally clear that a *temporal break* occurs in the second chapter of Genesis. This change in orientation and phraseology represents *a shift to a new frame of reference.* (I should note that while I identify Genesis 2:4 as the point of temporal departure, Schroeder believes this break in orientation, which clearly does occur, is actually represented better by Genesis 2:7 where God breathes into Adam's nostrils the "breath of life.")

Certainly, as this Schroeder-Lefavi model demonstrates, the second chapter of Genesis contains the point in early scripture where time begins to be described from a new vantage point, an Earthly vantage point, thereby providing *harmony to the creation account* (both before and after that point) and allowing science and spirituality to stand side-by-side when describing it.

Despite today's societal tendency to deny the important and active role of anything spiritual, the more we learn about the world, the better we can see that the age-old scriptural description of creation is increasingly likely. As science-historian Frederick Burnham said after the COBE (NASA satellite Cosmic Background Explorer) observations of 1992, in which scientists came to a nearly unanimous view that the universe originated at one definite point, "These findings, now available, make the idea that God created the universe a more respectable hypothesis today than at any time in the last 100 years."

*Beyond Fundamentalism*

Once again, it should be clear that I am not a scriptural literalist and I'm not out to prove the veracity of the Bible–the Bible can take care of itself. Of course any time people make a solid case for scripture-science (or scripture-world) harmony, they are hung out to dry as fundamentalists. While I believe that properly understood scientific findings and a properly understood Bible produce consistency, it misses my point to focus on what, if any, "category" the messenger of the harmony should be placed in. By shunning reasonable discourse on the harmony between science and spiritual tenets, we remove the most important scriptural text the world has ever known from that which we call "real," relegate it to nothing more than myth, and keep our spiritual sense–the core of our true relationship with God–from awakening and growing.

## Evolution and the Creation: Design and Intervention

> The likelihood of the formation of life from inanimate matter is one to a number with 40,000 noughts [zeros] after it.... It is big enough to bury Darwin and the whole theory of Evolution.      –British astronomer Sir Fred Hoyle

The evolution of humankind following the creation of life is the other major question in the creation dilemma that brings about conflict, dissonance and spiritual denial within individuals and, ultimately, society. Even today this issue stirs intense emotions and is responsible for controversy everywhere from the media to school board meetings.

*Darwin's Evolution and the Process of "Making"*

"Evolution" is a process that results in heritable changes in a population spread over many generations. For my purpose, I will use the term evolution to mean both micro-evolution (population and species change over time) and macro-evolution (general evolution: progression to more complex forms of life).

Upon hearing any discussion of evolution, most people today think of Charles Darwin who published his pivotal *Origin of Species* in 1859. In this revolutionary book Darwin provided insight into the mechanics of evolution, proclaiming that every population of creatures always has a great deal of variation (stemming from mutations in genetic material) – more feathers, more attractive to the opposite sex, less visible to predators, and so on – and that some of these variations allow the creatures bearing them to thrive. In a competitive environment, Darwin explained, those fortunate creatures will have more and healthier offspring for longer periods of time than those not having the favorable variations. After many generations, these traits become more common in the population as a whole and thus develop over a period of time as the dominant trait.

Evolution, for Darwin, was driven by something he called "natural selection," the specific process of retaining the favorable trait and thereby causing the population to advance. This meant that advantageous mutations under conditions of competition proliferate and slightly alter species in the long-term.

It should be pointed out that, for some, even the existence of these favorable mutations appears unlikely, though for the sake of argument I will assume they can and do occur. For example, Pierre-Paul Grasse, past-president of the French *Academie des Sciences,* wrote in *Evolution of Living Organism:*

> The opportune appearance of mutations permitting animals and plants to meet their needs seems hard to believe. Yet the Darwinian theory is even more demanding: a single plant, a single animal would require thousands and thousands of lucky, appropriate events. Thus, miracles would become the rule: events with an infinitesimal probability could not fail to occur.... There is no law against day dreaming, but science must not indulge in it.

Scientists, as well as experts in scripture, seem to agree that, like the creation of the universe, the "making" of humankind took time and many processes; no single event "made" humankind. In fact, scientist Roy Clouser has written that the Biblical account of humankind being made "is not to be understood as teaching that God made a mud model of a life form with no biological predecessors and blew on it with the result that it came alive, hopped up and walked around."

Unfortunately for all, that's where the agreeing ends.

### Fat Chance for Life

> Molecular evolution is not based on scientific authority. There is no publication in the scientific literature in prestigious journals, specialty journals or books that describes how molecular evolution of any real, complex, biochemical system either did occur or even might have occurred. There are assertions that such evolution occurred, but absolutely none are supported by pertinent experiments or calculations.
>
> Michael Behe in *Darwin's Black Box*

It may be a surprise to many, as it was to me, that there is *no* adequate explanation for the origin of life from dead chemicals. Even the simplest form of life is tremendously complex. At best, the early Earth would have contained a primeval "soup" of chemicals, though many biologists insist there is no evidence for even this to have existed. Assuming that an ideal mix of chemicals *was* present, for life to have been produced (which some scientists call chemical evolution as distinct from biological evolution), simple organic molecules must have been assembled into large macromolecules such as protein, DNA and RNA, a process which requires a considerable amount of energy.

In this process, along with other components of life such as lipids, carbohydrates and enzymes, one would have needed a molecule called "cytochrome c" with the correct sequence of 101 L-amino acids (the proverbial "building blocks" for protein). The chance that proteins basic for life appear simultaneously would occur twice in 10 to the 94th possibilities (that number is a "1" with 94 zeros after it). The *perfect best-case scenario,* with all the right catalytically active protein molecules in close proximity, assuming all the nonfunctional amino acids and other reacting compounds present did not get in the way for some strange reason, would have these necessary proteins appearing twice in 10 to the 65th possible events.

Even the famous astronomer Sir Fred Hoyle, himself an atheist, calculated the probability of life forming by chance in five billion years on Earth as being a number so close to zero as effectively being zero. He then assumed a best-case scenario with a universe containing 100 billion galaxies each with 100 billion stars and 20 billion years. Still he found no real chance of life forming. In his book *The Intelligent Universe,* Hoyle said that the present scenario of the origin of life forming anywhere in the universe is as likely to have occurred as a tornado sweeping through a junkyard next to the Boeing airplane company and accidentally assembling a 747!

In 1968 Yale physicist Harold Morowitz published *Energy Flow in Biology* where he presented computations on how unlikely it would be to form life on Earth from random chemical reactions. Instead of trying to form human life from the entire age of the Earth (4.5 billion years), he went further. First he assumed very fast rates of chemical reactions, then he showed that random reactions could not account for the production of bacteria in 4.5 billion years, they couldn't even produce *bacteria* in the 15 billion years of the entire universe! There was simply not enough time for life to emerge from dead matter.

*Too Much, Too Quickly.* To give you a better handle on this, I should explain that the oldest sedimentary rocks unearthed are in the southern African shield and the Canadian shield and are 3.8 billion years old. As mentioned, researchers discovered fossils of microbial life forms in early sedimentary rock in Africa and Australia dated at about 3.5 billion years old, not even half a billion years younger than the rocks themselves. Fossil records show that the earliest evidence of life with the appearance of a genetic code is dated at about 2.8 billion years ago. That's only 1.7 billion years after the Earth was formed and 0.7 billion years after the earliest single-celled organisms appeared! Forget about improbability; for all intents and purposes it is *impossible* to produce such complex life forms from random chemical reactions in such a brief period of time.

In fact, it is so statistically unlikely for random events to have produced life such a short time after the Earth was able to host life that Nobel laureate and agnostic Francis Crick, along with Fred Hoyle, has gone so far as to search the skies for ways life could have come to Earth from other parts of the universe. Even Crick agreed that "the origin of life appears to be almost a miracle, so many are the conditions which would have to be satisfied to get it going."

As Hubert Yockey wrote in the *Journal of Theoretical Biology,* "One must conclude that, contrary to the established and current wisdom, a scenario describing the genesis of life on Earth by chance and natural causes which can be accepted on the basis of fact and not faith has not been written."

In short, too much happened too quickly. Overwhelming fossil evidence does not confirm, temporally, a random, gradual evolution of life—not without some force directing it or pushing it along.

*The Hand of God*

"Survival of the fittest" and "natural selection." No matter what phraseology one generates, the basic fact remains the same: any physical change of any size, shape or form is strictly the result of purposeful alignment of billions of nucleotides (in the DNA). Nature or species do not have the capacity for rearranging them, nor adding to them. Consequently no leap (saltation) can occur from one species to another. The only way we know for a DNA to be altered is through a meaningful intervention from an outside source of intelligence: one who knows what it is doing, such as our genetic engineers are now performing in their laboratories.
—I.L. Cohen in *Darwin Was Wrong: A Study in Probabilities*

We are faced more with a great leap of faith that gradual, progressive adaptive change underlies the general pattern of evolutionary change we see in the rocks than any hard evidence.
—Eldredge & Tattersall, *The Myths of Human Evolution*

There is yet another way in which fossil records support intervention—the absence of "transitional forms" of life in the fossil record. Transitional life forms should appear *between* the various distinct types of organisms uncovered in the fossil record if slow, gradual evolution did occur. That is, there should be a fossil record of the gradual conversions. Scientists should be able to take fossils and assemble them into a series of life forms showing minor changes in species as they evolved. But there is no such record.

Instead, fossil records provide evidence of large, very rapid changes in species, separated by long periods of little or no change. Specifically, very distinct organisms, appearing fully-formed when first present, displaying no real direct connection to the species that immediately predated them and with clearly defined gaps between them, make up the fossil record. For example, insects appear already developed without ancestors. Flies are flies, cockroaches are cockroaches with no common ancestors, nor is there any ëssil record showing how they were able to develop the ability to fly (no "intermediates").

As one might imagine, this abrupt appearance of new life exhibiting sudden, large jumps between forms of life is not very consistent with Darwin's evolutionary flow of gradual selection from spontaneous mutations in a competitive environment. As renowned biologist Ernst Mayr wrote,

> What one actually found was nothing but discontinuities. All species are separated from each other by bridgeless gaps; intermediates between species are not observed. . . . The problem was even more serious at the level of higher categories.

Likewise, Tom Kemp writes in *New Scientist*,

> Each species of mammal-like reptile that has been found appears suddenly in the fossil record and is not preceded by the species that is directly ancestral to it. It disappears some time later, equally abrupt, without leaving a directly descended species.

Moreover, even in the unlikely event that intermediate forms did briefly exist, these incipient stages would not be of help to the species. As scientist Soren Lovtrup explains in *Darwinism: The Refutation of a Myth*,

. . . the reasons for rejecting Darwin's proposal were many, but first of all that many innovations cannot possibly come into existence through accumulation of many small steps, and even if they can, natural selection cannot accomplish it, because incipient and intermediate stages are not advantageous.

Today more than ever, scientists are questioning conventional and orthodox Darwinism—evolution through natural selection with no other intervention or force involved. For me, it was interesting to realize that the more science uncovers, the less likely it seems that Darwinian evolution occurred. We should think carefully before removing from the picture the idea of a higher power and "purpose." Of course, any proof of such an intervention, if it were to be discovered, would not at all indicate that evolution didn't occur. Clearly *it did*.

Humankind *did* "evolve" from ape, under the control and direction of a higher power in the process of "making" that both science and scripture describe. At a particular point, scripture shows, God and humankind began a more intimate relationship and not only was the "creation" of Adam and Eve actualized, but also the ape continued along a separate line (with today's human having 46 chromosomes and today's ape having 48).

I am not the only one among the many who have studied the origin of life to be convinced of God's role in evolution. Many scientists now believe deeply in "creative design," a process that acknowledges the age of the Earth and the fossil record while accepting that everything in creation is a product of intelligent design, not blind chance. Certainly, this view, even from a scientific standpoint, fits the evidence better.

*The Same Mountain*

Unfortunately, zealots still enjoy pitting one side against the other. I recently saw a church marquee that read "Evolution is a Kong-size lie." How absurd! Do these people really expect scientists simply to ignore hard evidence? That's no way to create an intelligent dialogue where both bodies of knowledge can learn from each other. Myopic, naïve assertions such as these keep many scientists from seriously and critically examining the validity of spiritual wisdom and God's involvement in the world.

Likewise, many scientists find it easier to label any rational argument against macroevolution as "religious creationist propaganda." Using this knee-jerk "us versus them" mentality precludes having to sit down and really think about the validity of a good argument. I know too many closed-minded scientists who refuse to give even one iota of credence to spiritual pursuits of reality.

Yes, there actually *is* harmony and a means for consolidation. The perception that the scriptural account of the creation of life is mutually exclusive from the scientific literature on the topic is unwarranted and the cognitive dissonance and subsequent intrapersonal and social spiritual denial arising from such a perception is unfortunate. Scientists and theologians are looking at the same mountain, just from different sides.

It seems to me that both camps of knowledge can and should stand side-by-side in the search for truth. Why not? What is there to lose? By remaining estranged from one another, both have a more difficult time clinging to irreproducible, untestable theories. As biologist L. Harrison Matthews writes, "Belief in the theory of evolution is . . . parallel to belief in special creation – both are concepts which believers know to be true but neither, up to the present, has been capable of proof." What I realized, however, is that by deeming one the "spiritual" explanation, we imply it is not real and stifle our ability to acknowledge and grow in spirituality.

## Reasonableness

When all I relied on for knowledge was data and what I could measure, I was as proud as any scientist could be to say that I used "reasonableness" as a guidepost when interpreting my findings. Later it seemed ironic to me that this reasonableness often goes by the wayside when scientists evaluate anything related to the spiritual realm.

For instance, the environment in which the subsequent creation occurred had to be *so precise* that any *reasonable*, rational-thinking person must agree there was some force or intelligence directing it; perfect coincidences speak to design. Admittedly, this is something I would never have been able to see had I not been vested in "reason" while seeking God.

Indeed, the more we uncover about the beginning of the universe and the creation of humankind, the more we see that it is much more *reasonable* to state that God exists and God is the natural lawmaker than to say that all this is the highly unlikely result of a cosmic crap-shoot. *Even in a science-based world*, the existence and reign of a higher power are the conditions more likely to be "real."

# 4

# Spirituality, "Connection" and Health

As it is not proper to cure the eyes without the head, nor the head without the body, so neither is it proper to cure the body without the soul. —Socrates

Life's short, pray hard. —Reebok's slogan, with a twist

Someday, after we have mastered the winds, the waves, the tides and gravity, we shall harness for God the energies of love. Then, for the second time in the history of the world [we] will have discovered fire. —Teilhard de Chardin

After reconciling the dissonance I had on the issue of creation, I was fascinated by studies clearly showing that a person's spirituality is of utmost importance in health and medicine. Researchers in health sciences, however, acknowledge and accept spiritual phenomena and answers more readily than do scholars in the natural sciences. This is probably due to the universal view that the body *incorporates* a spirit.

Until only two decades ago the pendulum of healthcare had been stuck on the side of physical medicine–drugs and surgery reigned. Medical practitioners and we in health research always gave lip service to the idea of optimal health being a balance of mind, body and *spirit*. Yet we often ignored the importance of the spirit in health and medicine, and focussed a tremendous amount of attention on promoting healthy lifestyles, teaching people what they ought to *do* physically for optimal health–eat less fat, exercise regularly, etc.

Although such behaviors promote health, what I have discerned revolves around two basic underlying ideas. First, there is something more to health that we're missing. Syme's work shows that in a group of people with three of the major cardiac risk factors–high cholesterol, hypertension and smoking–over the next ten years four out of five of them will *not* have a heart attack! Even considering the effects of genetics and environment, we're still missing something. Second, perhaps what we are missing is, in part, something we already possess but have simply lost sight of. Maybe what we have forgotten is the spirit, that health is as much a matter of our spiritual *being* (our eternal selves) as it is a matter of our physical *doing*.

*Fortunately,* we're seeing a renewed interest in the beliefs and practices that link health with spirituality. In fact, this new attention to spiritual health is occurring in precisely those sectors of American society we think would only rely on conventional approaches to healing–educated, upper middle-class, urban and suburban dwellers.

What I have found, and what follows, is a fascinating look at how spirituality *interacts* with health. Specifically, I'll discuss the health and medical research pointing us to many *subdimensions* of spirituality. You'll see that we've denied the importance of the spirit in healthcare for far too long.

# Belief in a Higher Power

. . . Faith in God, in particular, has many positive effects on health.      — Herbert Benson, MD, in *Timeless Healing*

Meaningless is equivalent to illness.      — Carl Jung

[God] is the restless breathing we still hear in our sleep.
      — Jack Miles in *God: A Biography*

No one can truly stand erect until they have first bent the knee to Almighty God.      — Unknown

## *Creed — The Cornerstone of Spirituality*

Certainly, "belief" that there is some creative force, a power greater than ourselves, providing order in the universe can often be a source of strength for many people having difficulty with mental or physical health. But is there something transcendent here, something intrinsic to this belief system that brings about good health as a function of the belief itself? Is God involved? Research seems to be pointing in that direction.

For example, Pollner at UCLA discovered that even after controlling for church attendance and sociodemographic background, a person's relationship with God had a significantly positive effect on several measures of psychological well-being. Likewise, a recent study found religious belief to be associated with a lower blood pressure among adults and that this relation was a direct one (versus an indirect relation, through physical activity and other health behaviors). Finally, and perhaps most interesting, are the results of a ten-year study by Columbia University and the National Institute for Healthcare Research that showed that daughters of women who are religiously committed are 60 percent less likely to have a major depressive disorder than daughters of women without such a religious commitment. When mother and child belonged to the same denomination, daughters were 71 percent less likely to suffer from major depression and sons were 84 percent less likely.

That belief is associated with protection from illness is especially apparent among the elderly. In examining 232 elderly post-cardiac surgery patients, Oxman and colleagues at Dartmouth-Hitchcock Medical Center established that, independent of social support factors, those who claimed at least some comfort from their religious feelings were three times more likely to survive in the critical six months following the surgery than those who received no comfort from religious faith. In addition, Zuckerman's group established that even when present health status, habits, gender, marital status and social contacts from church were considered, religiousness was significantly correlated with lower mortality in elderly people.

Carl Jung explained how important a person's belief is to mental health when he wrote:

> Among all my patients in the second half of life–that is to say, over 35–there has not been one whose problem in the last resort was not that of finding a religious outlook on life. It is safe to say that every one of them fell ill because he had lost what the religions of every age have given to their followers, and none of them has been really healed who did not regain his religious outlook.

I believe it is not "religion" per se that enhances health but rather that a person's mental and physical health can be optimized as a result of spiritual awakening and growth. This growth manifests itself in changes in a person's heart and, though not necessarily, often in a context of religious searching and practice. I believe people who are religious *are* more likely to be spiritual–opening their hearts to a loving relationship with God and feeling a sense of personal capacity and longing to do good. It is through these inner manifestations of spirituality that one can change internally and externally, becoming happier and having lower anxiety and a more positive outlook.

*Transcendent Grace?* Even beyond these somewhat identifiable changes, may there be something intangible that occurs with belief that facilitates healing and recovery? If so, could these positive changes be a kind of transcendent grace from God? I find it incredibly interesting that, despite tremendous advances in medical science, the single most effective treatment we have for an alcoholic is the Alcoholics Anonymous (AA) program. What is AA but a program based upon a step-by-step process of *spiritual growth,* complete with a surrender to and reliance on a higher power for assistance? *How* does AA do it?

Programs such as AA help "addicts" admit that (a) their lives have become unmanageable, (b) a higher power can restore them to wholeness, and (c) they can change their destructive behavior by *turning their will and lives over to the higher power.* *Why* does the concept of a higher power help in this recovery? I do not know; I know only that it does.

## The Hopeful Heart

Some researchers in behavioral medicine feel that belief in a benevolent higher power creates a potent reason for hope and optimism and that these outlooks have physiological benefits. From a health standpoint, I do not believe that hope is a Peter Pan sort of concept where one ignores difficult circumstances. Rather, the attitude of hope is a choice a person makes in spite of difficult circumstances. It is for this reason that I liken hope to a form of courage.

Researchers have come to find that hope and optimism may affect physical health and the progression of illness. A study reported in the *Lancet* described 57 women who were diagnosed

Reasons to Believe

with early breast cancer and who were placed in one of three groups based upon their mental attitudes—a "stoic accepter" group, a "hopeless/helpless" group and a "fighting spirit" group. After ten years, 25 percent of the stoic acceptors were alive, 20 percent of the hopeless/helpless patients were alive, and 70 percent of the fighting spirit group were alive!

In another study, Schmale and Iker interviewed a number of women who were admitted to a hospital for a cervical biopsy. Each woman was rated according to the amount of hope she had. When the biopsy results came in, the findings were surprising: of the 18 women who lacked hope, 11 were diagnosed with cancer, of the 33 who were brimming with hope, only seven were diagnosed with cancer. Moreover, Green and Green examined 400 cases of "spontaneous cancer remission" and discovered only one factor common to each case—a change of attitude to one of hope and positiveness prior to remission.

Where does this hopeful attitude come from? It would seem that spiritual searches and a heightened awareness of God can give one hope and optimism. Goddard's research, which ascertained that almost two-thirds of the patients interviewed stated that faith, spirituality, religion and belief in life after death gave them hope, supports this. It is this "spiritual hope," in which hope is a function of faith in a higher power, compared to what may be called "secular hope," a sort of mind-over-matter pridefulness the modern world embraces, that research shows enhances mental and physical health.

Thus health research shows that hope and optimism might be mechanisms through which belief can have physiological benefits. Even Carl Sagan, not particularly known for his support of spiritual pursuits, said, "Within strict limits, it seems, hope can be transformed into biochemistry."

*Purpose in Life*

Individuals with a strong sense of purpose—the meaning ascribed to one's actions and life—often have come to grips with their own mortality and look forward to each day. It is like the story of the three stonecutters, each chipping away at a large block. A passerby approaches the first stonecutter and asks, "Excuse me, sir, but what are you doing?" The stonecutter replies rather gruffly, "Can't you see? I'm chipping away at this big hunk of stone!" Asking the second stonecutter the same question, the worker replies to the passerby with a grin, "I'm earning a living to support my wife and children." Moving to the third worker, the passerby asks, "And what are you doing?" This stonecutter looks up, face beaming, and says with reverence, "I'm building a cathedral!"

I believe a person's sense of purpose in life becomes apparent when God, through grace, reveals it. This revelation, I have seen, occurs when people tap into and seek to nurture their spiritual sense and *relationship with the divine.* Thus, faith is integrally tied to "purpose." As psychologist John Teske wrote, "The real promise of faith is not that we will live forever, but that our lives will have meant something when the sands of time run out." It is this sense of purpose that helps a person live with clarity and vitality. The Austrian psychiatrist Victor Frankl wrote, "Nothing is more likely to help a person overcome or endure troubles than the consciousness of having a task in life."

However, a sense of purpose might not only help create a meaningful, fulfilling life, it also might empower one to withstand the mental and physical stresses of life—stresses which often take their toll on one's health. Having survived the insanity and brutality of the Nazi death camps in World War II,

Frankl observed there was a factor beyond intellect or psychology that enabled some people to retain their humanity and survive in inhumane circumstances. This factor, he concluded, was "meaning" – purpose, a capacity to find through deep dialogue with one's self a positive significance in the events of life.

Consistent with this, study after study on the psychological factors of people who survive the death of their spouse shows that those who have something or someone to live for (God's purpose for them, and so on) not only survive for a longer period of time than those without such a purpose, but they also enjoy better health for the remainder of their life.

## Being Loving and Good

> It is this intangible thing, love, love in many forms, which enters into every therapeutic relationship. And it is an element which binds and heals, which comforts and restores, which works what we have to call – for now – miracles.
> – Karl Menninger in *The Vital Balance*

> When I reviewed the scientific literature, I was amazed to find what a powerful difference love and relationships make on the incidence of disease and premature death from virtually *all* causes. – Dean Ornish, MD, in *Love & Survival*

*Love and Connection: The Ultimate Manifestation of Spirituality*

Over the past two decades researchers in the health sciences have begun to talk about the protective effects of "connection." This term refers to what you might think – intimacy, closeness and a sense of belonging in a loving relationship. Although scientists in behavioral medicine use the term "connected," I could just as accurately call this power "love" because love is an internal force that unites and connects people in intimacy and closeness. Love and connection (or whatever you call it) are the ultimate manifestations of spirituality. They require an open heart and open arms. Only then can health-promoting connection occur. Results from several studies provide evidence of this relation between connection and health.

In one investigation of more than 7,000 adults in Alameda County, California, and another of 13,000 men and women in Finland, researchers established that, independent of all other cardiac risk factors, those individuals who had the fewest social contacts also had a two to three times greater risk of death from heart disease than those who had the most social contacts. Additionally, at Yale University's School of Medicine, 119 men and 40 women completed a psychological questionnaire and underwent coronary angiography, a test to find blockages in vessels around the heart. Again, independent of all other risk factors such as age, sex, hypertension, cholesterol level and smoking, the more people felt loved and supported, the less blockage they had in their coronary arteries at angiography.

In another study of 2,700 adults in Tecumseh, Michigan, investigators reported that not only were socially involved people (mostly volunteers in community organizations) more likely to be in the best health, but that when social ties were interrupted or broken, the incidence of disease increased significantly – especially ailments like coronary heart disease, strokes, cancer, arthritis, upper respiratory infections and mental illness. Researchers in this study concluded that "interrupted" social ties actually seemed to depress the body's immune system.

Experimental support for connection was made by Jay Kaplan and colleagues from Bowman Gray School of Medicine who studied cynomolgus monkeys – animals who are aware of and have social organizations much like people. They verified that though diet and activity levels were controlled, monkeys who were socially isolated had twice the atherosclerotic plaque (coronary blockage) as those who were allowed to live together.

Evidence also exists of the benefits of connection following illness. A Yale University study tracked 2,806 men and women aged 65 and older. Among the 194 who had heart attacks, some 59 died soon after their attack. Those with at least two sources of emotional support before their heart attack were twice as likely to survive as those with little or no emotional support.

Consistent with this concept of connection, intimacy and support, marriage as an institution/sacrament appears to be protective. James Goodwin and colleagues at the Medical College of Wisconsin found unmarried people with cancer had lower overall survival rates, even after adjustments were made for disease severity and type of treatment.

Further, researchers at the University of California, Davis, reported in 1990 that married people have healthier immune systems than the unmarried. In numerous studies married people have been shown to have lower rates of heart disease, accidents, alcoholism, cancer, hypertension and suicide than single people—in general they even live longer than the unmarried.

So important are love, connection and intimacy to physical health, and so interesting are the implications of it to science, spirituality and society, I'd like to describe more closely this health safety net. What follows is a description of what I call the four Cs of connection—communication, contact, community and crisis—all of which promote health-enhancing intimacy.

*Communication.* Connection is fostered by talking and sharing. David Spiegel of Stanford's School of Medicine, a self-proclaimed skeptic about the power of connection, divided 86 women with terminal cancer into two groups: one received standard medical care, the other received the same care but also met in a support group to talk. Keep in mind that no medical information was given in the support sessions; subjects simply came together to talk about their feelings and experiences.

Spiegel was shocked to find that of these women – all "terminal" cancer patients – those not meeting in a support group survived an average of only 19 months, while those in the support group survived an average of 37 months – nearly twice as long. After this work was published in the *Lancet* Spiegel said, "Believe me, if we'd seen these results with a new drug, it would be in use in every cancer hospital in the country today!"

Pennebaker and colleagues at Southern Methodist University showed that sharing feelings boosts the immune system. They asked 25 adults to spend 20 minutes a day writing details about disturbing, traumatic events in their lives and describing their feelings. A control group spent the same amount of time writing about superficial topics. Blood tests revealed a strikingly improved immune function in the self-disclosing group, yet no such change in the control group. Six months later, the self-disclosers still showed positive health benefits. In their report, this research team wrote: "Failure to confide traumatic events is associated with long-term health problems."

In another study Pennebaker and Susman investigated the effects of connection on health following one of the most traumatic and stressful events anyone can encounter – the death of a spouse. In studying those whose spouses had recently died, they determined that those who bore their grief alone had a higher than average rate of illness while those who could talk about their feelings with someone had no increase in illness.

I believe connection enhanced through communication is one reason why psychotherapy (and even "confession") can be so helpful for some people. That is, where there is communication and connection, there is often trust – and trust can create an environment in which therapy becomes effective. Thus to a certain extent we all have an ability to facilitate some type of healing in those with whom we communicate and connect.

## Contact

Another way one can foster connection is through physical contact – touch. A fascinating study was done by researcher Robert Nerem in relating connection and touch to health. He was interested in the extent to which high cholesterol diets cause arterial blockage around the heart so he took a large group of genetically similar rabbits and put them in cages, one by one, along a wall. After feeding them all the same high-fat diet, he confirmed upon autopsy that most of the rabbits had what he expected – a significant amount of blockage. However, one particular group of rabbits showed virtually no blockage. What made it more interesting to Nerem was that all the rabbits who had very little blockage were in the bottom cages.

On further investigation he discovered that his lab assistant, a short woman, would pet and cuddle the rabbits in the lower cages when feeding them because she could reach them. When she fed the rabbits in the rows on top, she could just reach high enough to give them their food and water so they were isolated and relatively ignored. Nerem was skeptical about the supposed cause of the difference in disease so he repeated the study, this time making sure the only difference between the groups was touch. He reproduced the same results and reported in the reputable journal *Science* that there was more than 60 percent less blockage and significantly less arterial damage in the rabbits who were touched and cuddled compared to those that weren't.

As is to be expected, the health of infants suffers when they don't connect through touch and physical affection. This has been shown in both humans and animals. Chapin's work as early as 1915 established a direct correlation between infant illness and the lack of love and physical affection given them. More recently, Shanberg at Duke proved that human touch is essential to the growth of a child. The absence of touch appears to depress growth hormone levels and leads to a "failure to thrive" syndrome.

Other studies have shown that premature babies who are massaged gain more weight per day, are more active, more responsive and are more likely to be sent home earlier than those who are not. Moreover, Coe at Stanford proved that separating infant monkeys from their mothers suppressed the infants' immune systems even under the best conditions of nutrition and sanitation.

The problem, I believe, is not that we fail to connect to our infants and children through touch, but that for some reason we think this physical need stops in childhood. Consider, for example, the famous cafe study of Jourard and colleagues who sat in cafes around the world observing how people of various cultures interacted with each other by recording the number of times per hour adults, socially engaged in conversation, casually touched each other (not romantically, but in a friendly sort of way as one might touch an arm or shoulder to comfort another). Results were astounding. The number of touches per hour in San Juan, Puerto Rico, was 180; Paris, France's rate was 110; Gainesville, Florida, two; London, England, zero!

All over Europe and Asia women and men alike touch, embrace and walk arm-in-arm, close friends connected by touch. But there are some cities in the U.S. where these acts could get a person beaten!

We are a touchless society and I believe this lack of connection may adversely affect our health. Touch, in the proper perspective, is *essential,* the need for which we never outgrow. I am ever more convinced that this specific need to connect to others may be as much spiritual as it is physiological or psychological—possibly by way of some transcendent healing force.

*Community.* A third way we connect is through our "community," which clearly has a strong basis in spiritual tenets. A community is defined as having four elements: (a) a sense of being a member, (b) a feeling of personal influence, (c) the fulfillment of needs, and (d) shared emotional concern.

How well the surroundings in which you live and work embody these elements may affect your health if the case of the township of Roseto, Pennsylvania, tells us anything. This is a community with a surprisingly low incidence of heart disease, about one-sixth the national average. (They also had much lower rates of ulcers, dementia and other common disorders.)

Researchers went to Roseto to investigate their lifestyle, expecting to find a population with a low-fat, vegetarian diet, exercising aerobically, and so on. Instead they discovered people who were just as overweight, sedentary and meat-loving as the rest of America. Investigators *did* identify *one difference* between this community – largely a population of Italian immigrants – and the average American community. They were like a tight-knit family – they helped each other out, watched over each other's children, got together on the weekends and had a strong sense of belonging and community.

Stewart Wolf of Temple's School of Medicine noted,

> There was a remarkable cohesiveness and sense of unconditional support within the community. Family ties were very strong. And what impressed us the most was the attitude toward the elderly. In Roseto, the older residents weren't put on a shelf; they were promoted to 'supreme court.' No one was ever abandoned.

Was this cardio-protection simply a function of good genetics? No. Years later when the community atmosphere and family traditions began to dissolve and Rosetans became more industrialized and individualized (that is, more "Americanized") researchers went back to Roseto and discovered it had achieved the American incidence of heart disease–same people, greater frequency of disease.

It is interesting to note another group of people with a strong sense of spiritual connectedness and community which enjoys extraordinary health. The Abkhasians in Soviet Georgia who, despite the former Soviet Union having the industrialized world's highest rate of mortality from cardiovascular disease, often live well into their 100s. Instead of finding the Abkhasians eating yogurt, which through commercialization is how you may remember them, researcher Sula Benet noticed the "boundless commitment and mutual aid characteristics of [these] families. The individual measures his worth in terms of his ties to each and every family member. The more ties he has with different people, the more important he is in his own eyes and in the esteem of others." When asked, the Abkhasians typically count 300 or more in their family.

Similarly Nobel Peace Prize recipient Archbishop Desmond Tutu speaks about the importance of communal harmony in one's spirituality–you are only a whole person through other persons. He calls this *ubuntu*, a term with no equivalent in Western languages, and describes it as warmth, compassion, generosity, hospitality and seeking to embrace others.

*Crisis.* Finally, we connect through crisis. Although there is little research on crisis leading to connection, most people intuit the truth of this. Families instinctively connect in an incredible fashion when someone is sick or dies. In my family, funerals appear to be the time when we all get together, share each other's grief, realize anew how much we all mean to one another, vow to stay in closer contact and then go our separate ways until, of course, the next crisis. Unfortunately, it is sometimes crisis that reconnects us to our spirit, reminding us of both the importance and power of connection and love.

Americans saw firsthand an incredible display of community, cohesiveness and connection in the days following the tragic Oklahoma City bombing. (Local newscasters mentioning a need for things like batteries at the site of the bombing, would literally minutes later have to announce, "Okay, please, no more batteries!"). The incredible outpouring of affection between people tied together solely by this crisis only underscores how easily we lose sight of the important, potentially health-promoting and life-enhancing properties of connection.

In pointing to crisis as times when we regain this lost sense of connection and closeness, M. Scott Peck wrote:

> I can guarantee you that this Saturday night there will be tens of thousands of old men in VFW and American Legion clubs drinking themselves silly, mourning the days of World War II. They will remember those days with such fondness because even though they were cold and wet and in danger, they experienced a depth of community and meaning in their lives that they have never since quite been able to recapture.

Researcher Joan Borysenko has said, "Pulling together creates tremendous bonds between people. It nourishes our collective souls."

*Connection Protection.* Thus, connection through communication, contact, community and crisis appears to have positive effects on mental and physical health. As David Spiegel says, "Being highly connected socially as compared to being isolated socially is as powerfully related to mortality as smoking or high cholesterol."

Dean Ornish, a physician, addresses this concept in his bestseller *Reversing Heart Disease:*

In short, anything that promotes a sense of isolation leads to chronic stress and, often, to illnesses like heart disease. Conversely, anything that leads to real intimacy and feelings of connection can be healing.

*Love*

Although I've addressed issues many researchers believe to be closely related to love, since some investigators have looked at the effects of love per se, I should address this also. Dostoyevsky's assertion, "I am convinced that the only hell which exists is the inability to love," takes on new meaning when you consider that in most religions hell and evil are represented by the complete absence of God or love.

Few would argue that the ability to experience love (to receive and express love) is important in determining one's spiritual joy and happiness, but can love also be important for a healthy life? Harvard researchers McClelland and Kirshnit believe the answer is yes. They discovered that subjects who watched movies about love had significantly increased levels of immunoglobulin-A in their saliva (one's first line of defense against upper respiratory infections) compared to those who watched films with no such love theme.

In addition, an interesting study done by Medalie and Goldbourt highlighted the possible relation between love and heart disease. They asked nearly 10,000 men with major risk factors for cardiovascular disease (high serum cholesterol, hypertension, high anxiety levels, etc.) to complete lengthy psychological tests in order to find the most accurate psychological *predictor* of *angina*—pain in the chest. The researchers monitored the subjects' reports of angina over the next five years. The single response on the tests which predicted angina more than any other was the answer "no" to the question, "Does your wife show you her love?" In fact, men who reported that they did not have a loving wife had nearly twice as much chest pain as those answering that they did.

Says physician Bernie Siegel in *Love, Medicine & Miracles*:

> I am convinced that unconditional love is the most powerful known stimulant of the immune system. If I told patients to raise their blood levels of immune globulins or killer T-cells, no one would know how. But if I can teach them to love themselves and others fully, the same changes happen automatically. The truth is: Love heals.

What's love got to do with it? Perhaps a lot. There may be more than a little truth to what the noted London psychiatrist R. D. Laing wrote in his book *The Politics of Experience:*

> What we think is less than what we know. What we know is less than what we love. What we love is so much less than what there is. And to this precise extent, *we are* much less than what we are.

*Connection at Every Level?* Okay, so the mind affects the body. That's no great revelation, right? Anyone who has ever experienced a nervous stomach knows that. Actually I'm going much further than that simple assertion that emotions can manifest themselves in cells. I'm suggesting that one's experience of giving and receiving love affects physiology at a cellular level, beyond a simple physical mechanism such as the release of a certain chemical into the bloodstream. Somehow our cells "know" love and that love is God's fingerprint on every one of our cells.

To explain my rationale for coming to this conclusion we need to return to the topic of physics. When Max Planck originated many of the theories of quantum mechanics, explaining that the universe is not made up of many individual things separated by space and time but rather it is made up of quanta that transcend space and time, he was really suggesting that ultimately all in the universe is one.

Likewise Bell's Theorem described a synchronized dance across space and time that subverts our cause-and-effect way of looking at the universe. He said each quantum (particle of light energy) has a partner somewhere that "knows" what the other is doing and changes to match the other *no matter where it is!* These physicists were clearly describing that there seems to be order and purpose in the universe; we can "trust" the universe.

Candace Pert, research professor at Georgetown University and former division head at the National Institute of Mental Health, was the first to recognize this transcendent physiological reality as a result of her groundbreaking research. Not only does Pert believe that there is a neuropeptide profile for every emotion, she also asserts that all cells have a "mind." That may explain why researchers now have evidence that organs transplanted from spouses and close friends, regardless of all other factors affecting organ rejection, are physiologically accepted by the host better than organs from strangers.

It is rather startling to note the similarity between present medical science, the new physics and what spiritual leaders have been saying for centuries–namely, that we are all connected and that there is harmony and healing in our unified "oneness." Perhaps this healing power of connection and love is to some degree a function of a return to the wholeness and oneness we all have with each other.

Albert Einstein once said, "The illusion that we're separate is an optical delusion of our consciousness." Physicist Erwin Schrodinger posits, "Mind by its very nature is a *singulare tantum.* I should say: the overall number of minds is just one." Likewise in his book *Critical Path,* R. Buckminster Fuller described a phenomenon he called "cosmic costing" as a function of the inherent oneness of everything in the universe.

*Forgiveness*

The capacity to forgive is one subdimension of spirituality where research has illuminated the importance of spiritual wisdom to health and wholeness. Two aspects of forgiveness arise: not choosing hostility and isolation (or "disconnectedness") and the act of forgiveness itself.

*Not Choosing Hostility and Isolation.* The impetus for the body of research related to "disconnectedness" grew out of the famous Framingham, Massachusetts, study which found that the so-called risk factors for coronary heart disease (high cholesterol, hypertension, smoking, physical inactivity, age, gender, obesity, diabetes and family history) account for barely 50 percent of its incidence. Looking for some other determinant, Rosenman and Friedman later identified a way of responding to life which they labeled "type A" behavior pattern as the primary psychosocial factor affecting heart disease.

As you may know, type As are characterized as hard-driving, aggressive, goal-oriented, competitive, over-achieving, impatient, often hostile and self-focused. They do more and more in less and less time. They talk fast, eat fast, walk fast and firmly believe their bank teller slows down on purpose every time they get in line. More to the point, type As often are alienated from others and feel a general sense of disconnection.

From a health standpoint, the problem with type A behavior is not the unusual idiosyncrasies that often come with it, but rather that it has been highly correlated with coronary heart disease in many well-controlled and replicated studies. Blumenthal and colleagues at the Duke Medical Center reported that more than 90 percent of patients with severe coronary artery disease were type A. Even large prospective studies showed type A behavior pattern as highly associated with heart disease.

So significant were these findings that both the National Institutes of Health in 1980 and an independent review panel for the journal *Circulation* in 1981 officially recognized type A behavior as a risk factor for heart disease equal to or greater than other known risk factors.

There were detractors—and not without reason. Little by little, studies began to surface refuting type A behavior as a cardiac risk factor. After all, our society encourages and rewards most type A behavior, so it can't be all that bad, can it? Studies show that the vast majority of CEOs are type As; are they all simply heart attacks waiting to happen?

We now have an answer to that and the answer is "no!" More recent research has helped both to clarify this issue and shed new light on the role certain emotions tied to spiritual wisdom play in health. It was discovered that being a type A is not in itself a risk factor for heart disease, it's being a *hostile* type A that's a risk factor.

In psychological studies of type As, research teams headed by Chesney, Dembroski, Diamond and Williams established that those type As who scored high in the category of hostility, rather than any other aspect of the type A behavior pattern, were much more likely to develop heart disease than those who scored low in feelings of hostility. Additionally, a 1988 Finnish study of nearly 4,000 men determined that those who had been placed in either a "most hostile" or "hostile" group based upon their hostility scores from a psychological test three years earlier, were substantially more likely to die from cardiovascular disease than those placed in a "least hostile group."

Moreover, two long-term studies with physicians and attorneys as subjects revealed similar results. In the study on physicians, 225 male doctors who'd completed the Minnesota Multiphasic Personality Inventory (MMPI) while they were in medical school were tracked for 25 years. At the end of this time researchers confirmed the incidence of heart attack as five times greater in doctors with high hostility scores compared to those scoring low in hostility. The study on lawyers was nearly identical – 118 law students who took the MMPI while in law school had their death rate tracked for 25 years. Those attorneys scoring in the top 25 percent of the index for hostility were 4.2 times more likely to die than their lower scoring classmates.

What I believe this recent work is telling us is that classical type A behavior is harmful only to the extent it causes one to become angry, hostile and *disconnected* to others. It is the experience and manifestation of hostility that appears to be the killer, not competitive, hard-driving, achievement-oriented behavior. As researchers at Duke realized, "It is hostility that is most toxic to the heart."

A fascinating new line of research has taken this issue a step further and discovered that while it is best not to experience anger and hostility, if they are felt, they should be expressed. Negative emotions may occasionally have their place so long as they are freely and safely expressed (in a socially acceptable manner). This research, focused on health problems associated with unexpressed emotions, has given rise to the description of the "type C" personality – the cancer personality.

Type Cs are described as having difficulty expressing feelings openly, being stoic and persevering with despair. In their book *Psychosomatic Aspects of Neoplastic Disease,* Kissen and LeShan describe cancer patients as ignoring their negative feelings, such as anger and depression. Other studies on the type C personality include Graves and Shaffer of Johns Hopkins who identified psychological profiles of people in early life and correlated them with later disease. Individuals originally classified in the "loner" group – those defined as people having emotionless exteriors and inner loneliness (also disconnected) – were 16 times more likely to develop cancer than the group described as "acting out/emotional" – characterized as people who both felt their emotions intensely and expressed them.

In another long-term study begun in 1946, Caroline Bedell-Thomas assessed the personality profiles plus the mental and physical health of 1,337 medical students, continuing for decades after their graduation. She was actually looking for psychological antecedents of heart disease, hypertension, mental illness and suicide, but needed a factor for comparison – one which she felt would have no association with these problems – so she added in cancer. The results were extraordinary for it was discovered that almost all the cancer patients had throughout their lives shown restriction in expressing emotion, especially emotions related to their own needs.

Larry LeShan's findings, from a retrospective, in-depth study of 71 "terminal" cancer patients, turned out to be nearly identical. He established that despair, usually associated with the loss of an important relationship, coupled with an inability to express hostile feelings, predated the disease in 68 of the 71 cancer patients, yet only in 13 of 88 non-cancer patients.

This growing body of research, showing the incidence of cancer to be highly correlated with tucked-away feelings and a general reluctance to express emotions openly, has led many researchers in psychoneuroimmunology to label cancer "the disease of nice people." If you think of the people in your life who've developed cancer, more likely than not you'll find they are, as Bernie Siegel has written, "proper and generous people . . . [who] put the needs of others ahead of their own."

So recent research is suggesting that hostility and unexpressed emotions, each of which requires that we choose to ignore our physio-psycho-spiritual need to connect lovingly to others, may be tied to both heart disease and cancer (our two biggest killers). Perhaps Woody Allen's comment in the movie *Manhattan* is as truthful as it is witty: "Well, I don't get angry, okay? I mean I have a terrible weakness. I can't express anger. That's one of the problems I have. I grow a tumor instead."

*Forgiveness Itself.* In my work of facilitating support groups for people in crisis, I have become acutely aware that forgiveness promotes recovery. However, it's not just crises that bring about the need for forgiveness. I've seen many people who haven't been through tragedies still go through their lives as if they're "walking wounded." There are many circumstances in life that require forgiveness. Perhaps one's internal wounds stem from a divorce, maybe one hasn't gotten over being fired years ago or perhaps it's more serious, such as being sexually abused by a trusted person. Whatever the cause, the fact is that we can't go through life without being hurt by someone or some group of people.

Research is beginning to show, however, that the spiritual tenet of forgiveness is related to optimal health. Can a person who has difficulty letting go of past hurts ever be completely healthy? Studies now suggest the answer is no; the ability to forgive appears to affect one's overall health.

Although angry people may feel more powerful when filled with revenge and hostility, actually they are not. Kaplan describes his surprise when he confirmed that one of the four major themes of the behavior pattern which carries a low risk of heart disease (type "B" behavior) is that these people learn to be more forgiving. Specifically, he claims they have learned to judge themselves and others less severely, which rendered them remarkably less angry and hostile.

Pettit determined that forgiveness led to a reduction in chronic pain, cardiovascular problems and violent behavior. Likewise, Strasser reported that physical health in older adults was positively correlated with the ability to genuinely forgive and feel differently toward that person.

Forgiveness also benefits our mental health. Freedman and Enright reported that incest survivors who underwent forgiveness-oriented interventions with a psychologist had higher levels of hope and lower levels of anxiety and depression than a control group. Other studies have shown that the forgiveness levels of young adults who felt love-deprived by their parents were associated with lower levels of anxiety and depression, higher self-esteem and more positive views of the parents.

Perhaps the most important benefit of forgiveness is that it restores a sense of personal power to the victim. If we're victimized, it's as if we're actually continuing to give "power" over ourselves to anyone we refuse to forgive—in essence we are allowing the offender to control our emotions. Thus we need to forgive so we can move forward in life. An unforgiven hurt binds us to a time and place we did not choose; it holds us trapped in a past moment and in old feelings. Health-enhancing closure can never truly take place. Forgiveness restores relationships, even when the person we must forgive is ourself.

We must remember that forgiveness is a pardon we give a person or a group without demanding restitution. It takes place *inside us* and does not depend on whether the offenders seek forgiveness (they may not even be alive). Thus forgiveness is more an inner action of the will than an external act.

But it's easier said than done. In working with people on this, I have encountered many who think forgiveness can never occur. My response is two-fold. First, we must realize that the person is being forgiven, not the act. Second, even if we're not willing to forgive now, it's a start to be willing to be willing. We don't need to know exactly how we'll achieve forgiveness, but it's a loving and courageous act of the will to change the one thing we can control – our attitude. In its essence, forgiveness is about getting our heart right with God (I believe this is where the return to wholeness takes place, for it is a spiritual renewal – and mind, body and spirit can heal).

Forgiveness epitomizes the spiritual dimension – that there is something greater that transcends the immediate (even pain). It is obeying God; it is an inner act of faith.

Consider the consequences of unforgiveness: It keeps us *estranged from God and gets in God's way of dealing with that other person.* If we don't forgive, it's like saying what that person did was more important than our relationship with God. Remember the Chinese proverb: "The one who pursues revenge should dig two graves." A Holocaust victim who lost his wife, child and parents to the Nazi death camps of World War II told researchers he forgave because he chose to not bring Hitler with him to America.

In families the cycle of emotional damage, scars and anger – often transmitted unknowingly from generation to generation – can be replaced with a cycle of understanding, compassion and forgiveness. People and families can heal.

In American society, we don't promote the spiritual subdimension of forgiveness as we should. Although I have focused on the healing power of forgiveness between individuals, what would happen if our society acknowledged and asked forgiveness for crimes against women, homosexuals, the abuse or neglect of children and for the insensitive way we regard much of humanity?

*Deed*

Researchers often describe altruism as an integral outcome in one's stages of spiritual growth. Philosopher Philip Novak writes that when a person moves into this stage,

One grows more sensitive to "other beings" and to "children of God" if only because the dominating noise of the old self-program no longer drowns out their concerns. It's not that new love is "added" as if by force or will, but that the inner reservoir of love, once dammed, now flows.

I believe Novak is referring to that knowledge of God within us that recognizes our universal connectedness and promotes our reaching out to others in love and compassion.

Psychologist Susan Trout writes, "Service begins as an inner process rather than an outer action." What is this inner action that initiates a life of service? It all starts with becoming aware of and reconnecting to our spiritual sense and God. "One's inner call to God is the call to live a life of love through service," Trout explains.

But what about physical health, does that improve as well? It seems so. Alan Luks tapped into this positive benefit of reaching out to others when doing research for his book *The Healing Power of Doing Good.* Luks describes the results of surveying thousands of volunteers across the nation. He found that the group he studied consistently reported better health than peers in their age group. Moreover, many said their health dramatically improved when they began their volunteer work.

### Worship, Prayer or Meditation

From a health perspective, worship, prayer and meditation enable a person to *exercise the spirit* as one might exercise the body. Extensive research, including the Alameda County study on over 7,000 adults, indicates that, all things being equal, people who are members of and attend a church or synagogue are less likely to be ill over time (particularly of heart disease, lung disease, cirrhosis of the liver and some cancers) than those who do not. In addition, according to Dr. David Larson, formerly a research psychiatrist for the National Institutes of Health, a review of 30 years of research on blood pressure shows that churchgoers have lower blood pressure than non-churchgoers.

In 1997 Strawbridge, et al., concluded from a 28-year study of 5,000 adults that mortality for those attending weekly religious services was almost 25 percent lower than for those attending less frequently. For women the mortality rate was reduced by 35 percent. These researchers also found frequent attenders were more apt to stop smoking, increase exercising, increase social contacts and stay married. Even after making allowances for other factors, a mortality difference was still clear.

A 1996 National Institute on Aging study of 4,000 elderly persons showed that those who attend religious services are less depressed and physically healthier than those who don't. Additionally, non-churchgoers have been proven to have a suicide rate four times higher than those who attend church regularly.

Koenig and colleagues reported that frequent religious attendance in 1986, 1989 and 1992 predicted lower plasma interleukin-6 (IL-6 is an indicator of immune function) levels in a sample of 1,718 older adults followed over the six years, perhaps explaining why frequent churchgoers appear to have both better mental and physical health than non-churchgoers. In a study of those living in religious versus secular kibbutzim in Israel, researchers identified clear morbidity and mortality advantages to those who led religious lives, even when compared with those in a tightly-knit community without religious focus.

Some may say that much of this is a function of social support, love, connection and stress buffering. I believe that this research shows that, from a spiritual standpoint, *belief in God and the cultivation of a spiritual life (expressed in worship) themselves promote health and healing.*

It would seem that in all these cases there may be a transcendent action involved, that prayer may act at a distance – in what many metaphysicists would call "nonlocality." Many physicians and scientists are uncomfortable giving credence to nonlocal forces because generally speaking we feel uneasy believing in things that interact in ways our five senses cannot perceive. Yet, we accept these forces in other areas of our life, although Isaac Newton's theory of gravitation was initially attacked by critics because it implied "action-at-a-distance" – a concept many feared would revive the "occult properties" of the Middle Ages. Since Newton, however, generations of scientists have tried zealously to help us feel comfortable with nonlocality through their descriptions of magnetic fields, electric fields, electromagnetic fields, morphogenic fields, and so on.

Perhaps nonlocal actions is what physician Randolph Byrd assessed during a study at San Francisco General Hospital when he randomly divided 393 patients admitted to a coronary care unit for bypass surgery, all similar in age and severity of disease, into two groups – a prayer group and a control group. His team recruited people from around the country to pray for each of the 192 patients in the prayer group; five to seven people per patient were asked to pray every day in any form. The 201 patients in the control group received no such treatment. This was a double-blind study, meaning both the patients and medical staff were unaware which patients were in which group.

Prayed-for patients suffered fewer complications following coronary bypass surgery in three areas: antibiotic requirements (three in the prayer group versus 16 in the control group); pulmonary edema (six versus 18); artificial respiration (zero in the prayed-for group versus 12 in the control group). Although the results were published in the *Southern Medical Journal*, I believe that had scientists derived such effects from a new drug, the manufacturer would have heralded it as a breakthrough in coronary care and put it on the market soon afterward.

However, this study was not the first to demonstrate positive health effects from prayer. Larry Dossey, MD, in his book *Healing Words* writes how astonished he was to find more than 100 published studies using good scientific methods "over half of which showed that prayer brings about significant changes in a variety of living beings."

Perhaps there is at least some truth to Mark Twain's statement, "God cures, and the doctor sends the bill."

## A Spiritual Resuscitation?

> Through my research, I became convinced that beliefs have physical repercussions . . . that the human spirit is relevant – indeed influential – in the treatment and prevention of illness.
> –Harvard physician Herbert Benson in *Timeless Healing*

Yes, modern medicine is missing something. With all the power over disease that the medical community has given us through drugs and surgery, it still has overlooked the potential spiritual power within the patient.

As with the natural sciences, we see that the removal of spirituality and God from that which we view as real, valid and important has fostered its continual denial by many who seek help only in medicine. In addition, as with the natural sciences, this denial has occurred relatively recently and creates a great deal of dissonance in the mind of any healthcare practitioner wanting to treat whole patients as well as with the patients who already are aware of and feel the power of the spirit.

Ironically, the pendulum of healthcare used to be balanced where health and healing were parts of religion and family, but contemporary medicine has separated itself from these two institutions. Modern medicine, particularly that which exists in America, focuses on diseases rather than on sick persons and has removed the care of persons from the context of their family. Daniel Wirth, director of Healing Sciences Research International in Orinda, California, writes:

> As the years progressed, medicine completely shifted its focus from a holistic spiritual assessment of individual patients to a science which gathered objective data on the universal aspects of disease pathology.

In the past century a division has taken place that relegates the care of a person's physical well-being to the medical profession and the care of a person's spiritual being to religious leaders. How unfortunate that some healthcare professionals don't recognize the spiritual needs of a patient since they are so closely involved with people during the more spiritually important times in their life – birth, death and crises. As health professionals David and Susan Larson and Glenn Wood write, "When patients are looking for spiritual comfort at a time of need, they might be shunted off to a psychiatrist lacking in faith, who places them on psychotropic drugs lacking in efficacy for a grieving soul lacking in comfort."

### Re-Centering the Pendulum

Many of us in the health sciences have been trying to re-center the pendulum of healthcare; many gains have been made in that direction. Even the most skeptical health professionals are beginning to see that what we are trying to achieve, optimal heath and well-being, is as much a matter of our spiritual being as our physical doing.

If you so desire, you can eat fiber until you turn into a brick, but the fact remains that people in the best health seem to acknowledge their spiritual sense – that knowledge of something greater than themselves. Researcher David Aldridge says,

We need to recognize that patience, grace, prayer, meditation, hope, forgiveness, and fellowship are as important in many of our health initiatives as medication, hospitalization, incarceration, or surgery.

Let me be clear that I do not relate these health benefits of spirituality to any form of "secular spirituality." I am in no way promoting a New Age, fluffy, "head-in-the-clouds" movement implying that we should abandon Western technological medicine, close our eyes, click our heels and wish away disease. American medicine is the best healthcare the world has to offer (God made doctors, too) and without medical science and research, doctors would still have leaches on their desks. Medicine in the modern world merely needs to resuscitate its spiritual heartbeat – that which includes God in the treatment plan.

We in the health professions must speak about the power of spirituality to our patients. We desperately need to assimilate the spiritual view of health into modern medicine. Today's ethical dilemmas in healthcare – DNA manipulation, equity in the provision of health services, the use of fetal tissue, assisted suicide, and so on – mandate a spiritual foundation. As biochemist Walter Hearn has written, "What is clear is that by dropping the God of the Bible from its conversation, institutional science has lost its absolute, transcendent basis for ethical judgments."

It is encouraging that some communities today that have not lost spirituality in medicine seem to feel more fulfilled. Simon Dein writes about the Lubavitch, a group of Hasidic Jews London who use the Rebbe (their spiritual leader) for spiritual guidance:

> For Lubavitch, healing involves control of disease and correction of any spiritual disorder associated with it. . . . To the extent that the Rebbe provides personal and social meaning for the experience of illness he is providing cultural healing.

## By What Force?

Since the evidence of the integral relation between spirituality and health is quite clear, the next question that kept reverberating in my mind after investigating this field was: Why do certain emotions, such as love, and specific actions, such as forgiving, worshiping, loving and connecting, appear to protect health, while others, such as hostility and isolation, seem to be destructive? In fact, if we accept the concept of natural selection, one could make the case that this is exactly what you would *not* expect. You would expect hostility to promote conquest and dominance and thus be *the characteristic selected for.* What is it that appears to promote love and connection and discourage anger and hostility?

My search into the spiritual realm of health has left me only one possible answer to this question. The answer is God. God wants us to love, connect, forgive and worship. God is pushing us in one direction–toward God–yet we live in a world that refuses to recognize God's involvement in our lives.

**5**

# Truth under the Microscope

"Where is the wise? where is the scribe? where is the disputer of this world? hath not God made foolish the wisdom of this world?" —1 Corinthians 1:20

As I progressed down the path of spiritual unfoldings, I began to see how science and spirituality view the world and even how they are often talking about the same things in different ways. I became convinced that we need *both* for a fulfilling life. We must, however, understand what each brings to our life.

## Proof And Truth

Even the Spirit of truth; whom the world cannot receive, because it seeth him not, neither knoweth him.
—Jesus of Nazareth (Jn 14:17)

While I had always put "proof" on a pedestal, I now see it as a human process; that is, proof is *relative*. Proof of an item in question depends on (a) what standard you're comparing it to (i.e., Descartes compared the obvious existence of God to proof he saw in geometry), and (b) the subjective feelings of the person making the comparison. As religious scholar Thomas King contends, "Any proof is based upon [compared to] that which we take without proof."

Truth, though it cannot always be proved, is *absolute;* it is not relative. Truth, by definition, is something that is true whether we believe it or not. *It does not depend on our consent.* Thus we do not create truth, we encounter it.

Not even the scientific method can claim to create truth. This method is only a tool that can be used wisely or blindly. Referring to medical scientists, researcher Paul Pearsall says, "They have mistaken the strength of their remarkable methodology for truth itself." About the scientists' fallible "truth," Candace Pert writes, "We must stop worshiping a dispassionate 'truth' and expecting the experts to lead us to it."

Despite this limitation, science has gotten the reputation of being the absolute truth-teller. I believe this occurs for two reasons: First, we grant science a mystique that it is an all-knowing, mysterious process led by courageous discoverers. Although the latter is often true, scientists are still fallible humans. Second, we tend to defer to this mystique because it serves us to do so. We want definite, concrete answers. We want our facts, "the truth," neatly packaged into easily digestible sound bites. We don't want to know about the assumptions, the educated guesses, the "confidence levels" or the theoretical foundations that often go with a claim. We want fast food science. (Interestingly enough, virtually this same critique which is applicable to science, can be applied to fundamentalist religion.)

# Limitations Abound

Professing themselves to be wise, they became fools.
—St. Paul in his letter to the Romans (1:22)

Adding to the "truth-seeking" dilemma in science, scientific researchers often use a *reductionistic* approach to problem-solving. In reductionism, a problem is taken apart in order to solve it. Scientists relying on reductionism view truths as hierarchical, with some being less fundamental than others. They believe that by knowing and identifying the components of a complex system, they can explain the entire system.

Reductionism is a cold, impersonal view that makes determinations about the whole by looking at its parts, identifying mechanistic processes and arriving at general theories. However, sometimes the whole is greater than or functionally different from the sum of its parts and pieces, and can only be understood by looking at the whole. Thus in the health sciences, researchers delve deeply into the cellular mechanism of serotonin receptors involved in eating disorders, while little attention is given to the patient who has a psycho-spiritual disorder as much as a physical disorder—and who is often crying out for love. While research itself is good, we must remember that we cannot take apart the radio in order to find the music.

Likewise, a good bit of fallacious thinking that can accompany a reductionist approach hinders reaching an accurate conclusion or the "truth" about a complex system. The most destructive fallacies in reductionism are of *purpose* and *control*. Too often reductionistic scientists feel they have mastered a system by discovering the what, where and how of the mechanisms, while losing sight of the fact they have not answered "why?" Scientific explanations usually end with some natural or ultimate physical law, but we must remember that there is always another question: "Why are there natural or ultimate physical laws at all? More specifically, what is their purpose?"

Why *should* there be a purpose? Scientists, philosophers and investigators seek explanations for things. That's what science is about – explaining something complex in simpler terms.

Why stop with the explanation of the parts? As William Grassie writes in *Science & Spirit,* "As we traverse the sequential changes in time-space and matter-energy that have brought us to the moment of consciousness, let us ask the question why. Is it so preposterous to think that the biophysical processes that gave rise to our purpose-seeking species might themselves be processes imbued with purpose?"

The reason we stop where we do is because it's easier; "why" requires much more work and is often unknowable. Let us not forget that we have left a question unanswered – the question that spiritual teachings focus on. We have not answered and cannot answer "why" with science.

Astronomer Owen Gingerich from the Harvard-Smithsonian Observatory, describes modern science as rejecting teleology (the *teleological* argument for the existence of God is that the *design and order* of the universe implies a purpose or direction behind it, and likewise, a final goal or end), and says that "it is unfashionable in scientific explanations today to even hint at purpose or design. . . . Reductionism is the name of the game."

The process of breaking down the phenomenon and determining the underlying working mechanistic pieces does not validate the origin or purpose of the pieces or the whole. That is, *discovery is not creation!* In this cause-and-effect world, it is only reasonable to assert that things are created and survive for a reason.

Scientists also explain systems they have reduced in ways that imply control. For example, they might figure out what mechanistically happens during a particular "miracle" so they can feel they have solved it. Of course, they can no more control or affect the miracle-making process after identifying the mechanism than they could before identifying it.

Here are a few examples illustrating what reductionism misses:

1. *The Real Question of the Big Bang.*

When I described the rift between science and scripture regarding the origin of the universe and humankind, I discussed the beginning until the time of Adam – but alluded to the Big Bang only as clock-starting time. That's because there is no rift between science and scripture regarding the Big Bang. Everything we know about the Big Bang seems to fit; science describing the necessary "singularity" (something that can only be described in imaginary terms) as an infinitely small point and scripture referring to that point as a mustard seed (the message being "as small as possible") exploding to a larger and larger creation.

Likewise, from Doppler Shifts in light and Edwin Hubble's evidence in the 1920s, scientists now generally recognize it as true that all the universe is and has been expanding since the beginning of time. Moreover, George Smoot's revolutionary discovery, described in his book *Wrinkles in Time,* that he found previously predicted variations in radiation measured in millionths of a degree which all but confirmed the prevailing idea that a Big Bang started the universe. Smoot's finding was called "the scientific discovery of the century, if not all time," by noted physicist Stephen Hawking.

Mainstream science accepts the Big Bang theory. In fact it is likely that only the philosophical implications – that something had to initiate the Big Bang – have kept all scientists from embracing this theory. As Robert Jastrow of Columbia University has written in *God and the Astronomers:*

For the scientist who has lived by his faith in the power of reason, the story [of the Big Bang] ends like a bad dream. For the past 300 years, scientists have scaled the mountain of ignorance and as they pull themselves over the final rock, they are greeted by a band of theologians who have been sitting there for centuries.

Succinctly, everything that begins to exist must have a cause; if it had a beginning, then it had a creator. So the question eluding science is not so much whether the Big Bang occurred, or where, or how, but *why* it occurred. Remember, science cannot explain at all why the Big Bang got started.

## 2. *Conditions for Creation—Against All Odds*

The Big Bang screams of divine intervention. During the Big Bang itself the universe had to be extraordinarily "flat" in order to keep its present near-flatness. According to astronomer Owen Gingerich the flatness required was one part in 10 to the 60th. Even the most minuscule departure from that would bend space one way or the other and nothing would be here.

Further, as we have seen, our universe is a very unlikely place for life to have occurred. It's not as if you just add water, stir and you've got life. Scientist Brandon Carter explains that nearly all stars, including our sun, have only a very narrow range of gravitational forces within them which enable them to exist. If these forces were off by just one part in 10 to the 40th, those stars would not exist, nor would any life forms depending on those solar stars for their existence.

These examples of how so many details had to have been so extraordinarily precise in order for the universe and life to exist and how such small changes in universal constants produce dramatic changes in the universe is known as the *Anthropic* principle (often used in the past to "prove" the existence of God). This principle led astronomer George Greentein to say,

As we survey all the evidence, the thought insistently arises that some supernatural agency, or Agency, must be involved. Is it possible that suddenly, without intending to, we have stumbled upon scientific proof of the existence of a supreme being? Was it God who stepped in and so providentially created the cosmos for our benefit?

William Paley asks this question another way. His famous argument suggests that if you're walking in the woods and come across a watch on the path, you don't conclude that the watch just assembled itself by coincidence, despite the fact that you can take the watch apart, examine every part of it and understand how it works. On seeing the watch on the path you correctly conclude it was designed by some higher intelligence.

We give so much power and credence to the mechanism— the parts—that we forget about purpose. Nobel Prize-winning physicist Steven Weinberg writes that "we cannot calculate the course of biological evolution, but we now know pretty well the principles by which it is governed." So even though we can know the mechanism, we cannot in any way control it or understand its purpose.

3. *On Chaos and Order.*

The Law of Increasing Entropy (one of the three physical laws of thermodynamics), states that systems flow from concentrated, organized forms of energy to random, disorganized forms. Yet in the universe, especially when looking at forms of life, we continually see exactly the opposite occur.

If the trend in universal systems is toward chaos and disorder, then how do we have order at all, not to mention increasing order? Why is there a flow in the opposite direction? Here as well, the best we can do is to identify the mechanism taking place. The question "why?" perplexes us.

4. *Disease, Purpose and Biology.*

In the health sciences we are very close to finding genetic links to alcoholism, depression, heart disease, suicide, cancer, addictions and other diseases. But we can only identify what happens in a disease, not the spiritual side of the disease—why it occurs or the "purpose" of it, if you will.

What if we find, as Candace Pert suggests, there is a neuro-peptide profile for every emotion? Might there also be a biological marker for forgiveness or repentance? If so, that would add much to our knowledge of spirituality in health. What if we find a particular part of the brain that is involved in spiritual experiences? Wilder Penfield, a pioneer in modern neuroscience, discovered an area in the right temporal lobe of the brain that seems to be involved in spiritual experiences. Dr. Jonas Salk, of polio vaccine fame, called this area of the brain our link to "cosmic consciousness." In addition, Melvin Morse, MD, refers to the right temporal lobe as the "circuit boards of mysticism."

Interesting? Yes. However, even by locating these biological markers and "mystical" parts of our brain, we are only identifying the mechanism through which the spiritual realm connects to us; how God does it, so to speak. We have not mastered or controlled it. Succinctly put, just because we find the process doesn't mean that God is out of the picture; we've simply developed a better understanding of how God works.

5. *God and the Star in the East.*

We know from astronomers there probably *was* a bright star in the East around the time historical records show that Jesus of Nazareth was born. However, just because astronomers have identified the celestial pattern the star was in and de-mystified how it shone so brightly doesn't supplant divine guidance! No, for we still have not answered "why" or "by whose hand?"

Atheists often refer to any criticism of the reductionism of science by saying theists create a "God of the Gaps" for anytime a question cannot be answered, theists produce God as the answer. This is a hollow argument for clearly science uses its share of "post hoc," fill-in-the-blank analyses. When confronted with difficulty in explaining the lack of transitional fossils in the paleontological fossil record, biologists proposed "punctuated equilibrium." This model uses "peripheral isolates," specific migration and better adaptation of these isolates to account for the lack of steady evolution. This "science of the gaps" is inconsistent with the scientific method, and at best attempts to explain a mechanism – no way does it describe purpose.

While that "purpose" is not the intent of science, we must acknowledge science's inherent deficiency and not give it more power and credence than it deserves. Thus, I suppose I'm not arguing so much for a God of the Gaps as I am arguing against excluding God when attempting to confront "why?"

## The God Theory

> The significance and joy in my science comes in those occasional moments of discovering something new and saying to myself, "So that's how God did it." My goal is to understand a little corner of God's plan.
> – Henry F. Schaefer, quantum chemist and Nobel nominee

> I want to know how God created this world . . . I want to know [God's] thoughts, the rest are details. – Albert Einstein

When discussing spiritual issues with scientists, I often find the strife between science and spirituality described as being between "rational, logical-thinking" folk and "blind believers," the latter needing a crutch to deal with the real world. This outlook concerns me, as it is ill-founded.

For example, there are many tenets accepted in science that scientists don't know much about, yet they are accepted as true. In fact, I would say today's scientists cannot come close to explaining a fraction of the phenomena in our universe. We are hanging on to this spinning Earth knowing very little about our own backyard, much less the rest of the universe and how it works. As H.L. Mencken said, "The cosmos is a gigantic flywheel making 10,000 revolutions per minute. Man is a sick fly taking a dizzy ride on it."

In addition, it seems to me that *for science blindly to ignore the wide variety of spiritual phenomena, with a long history of at least circumstantial and anecdotal evidence supporting them, all in the name of "science" and simply because they may be unprovable at the moment, is in itself unscientific.* Earle Fox, who received an Oxford University doctorate on the relationship between science and theology, has written, "The scientific arena is where all (yes, even the religious) viewpoints are given equal opportunity to express themselves – so that the truth can be discovered."

Moreover, it is fair to say that "faith" grounds and guides scientists as well as spiritual scholars. The latter use scripture as the primary standard in testing their understanding of God's nature and activity, while scientists use data as the standard in testing theory.

Having stated the above and presented evidence to show how scripture supports the real world that science attempts to uncover, let me form these ideas into a "theory" (I use the term "theory" to give it credence in the modern world and so it can be discussed rationally) based upon the following issues that seem to me to be sound and reasonable.

First, science and spirituality base their propositions in a very similar manner. Second, a theory, unless a contradiction has been found to disprove it, must be assumed true in order to be investigated further. Third, theories pertaining to the creation of the universe and life without the assistance of another force are so unlikely as to be virtually impossible. Fourth, this book describes a genuine way scientists and spiritual thinkers can talk about the universe and creation – clearly the largest rift between the scientific and spiritual camps – intelligently without one group denigrating the other.

Then, *a fortiori* (an argument from the stronger position), consider "The God Theory": *A higher power, in close contact with humankind, has created (in 6 days and 15 billion years – Schroeder-Lefavi model) and directs the universe and life through concrete laws which science has been identifying since the beginning of recorded history. This higher power has given us all a spiritual sense which God wants us to be aware of and to nurture. God deeply desires our spiritual growth and encourages us to love others and lovingly worship God.*

This theory, though it might not fit the pattern of a typical scientific theory, is a concept that certainly qualifies as a possible answer to Einstein's search for a Unified Theory or the quests of today's scientists for a Theory of Everything – whose principles cannot be explained in terms of deeper principles.

The God Theory does not cast a shadow on science; rather it elevates spiritual pursuits of knowledge as powerful. It attempts to reconcile the last split between what have become competing and diverse but necessary bodies of knowledge. It is a theory that allows scientists and spiritual scholars to stand side-by-side in order to better serve the world. Intrapersonally, the God Theory could help us overcome the denial of God and the resultant cognitive dissonance that hinders our spiritual awareness and growth.

So what are we to do with such a theory? Teach the God Theory in school along with evolution? Although that is not my purpose here, I frankly see no reason not to. Why not give children *all* the knowledge we currently have? Why purposely avoid an acceptable theory that can give credence to very important sources of knowledge about life and the universe?

Schroeder's principles, based upon Einstein's work, and my subsequent small refinement, resulting in the science-spirituality harmony described in this book, can and should be used to *open serious discussions, using science and acceptable, reasonable theory, on the inclusion of spiritual tenets in the creation of the universe and life.* Are we so intimidated by the naturalistic, scientific world that we'll avoid seeking *all* truth so we don't appear too "religious"? If we do that, what personal and social price do we pay in the resultant cognitive dissonance and spiritual denial?

When it comes to presenting all known theories on creation to our young people, they can handle it; they're smarter than we take them for. If teenagers can go through metal detectors at school, confront drug use and go off to die for this country, aged 18, they can handle a little complexity in their lives and can make sense of the mixture! Anyone would agree that our children should have every opportunity to see the harmony between the "real" empirical world they live in and knowledge related to a higher power which is the essence of their being.

## Blind Faith?

Now faith is the substance of things hoped for, the evidence of things not seen.                              —Hebrews 11:1

Faith's what you find when you're alone and find you're not.                              —Political hostage Terry Anderson

It is precisely because I believe theologically that there is a being called God, and that God is infinite in intelligence, freedom, and power, that I cannot take it upon myself to limit what God might have done.—Fr. Theodore Hesburgh

In my search for answers about true spirituality, I realized that the concept of a benevolent, higher power who created the universe and humankind for a specific purpose is the only thing that truly makes sense and fits. Does anyone with half a brain really think this all happened by accident, that we're on our own? Summarizing the recent discoveries of many scientists, Robert Herrman, author of *The God Who Would Be Known*, says, "Everywhere you look in science, the harder it becomes to understand the universe without God."

For anyone with a sense of true spirituality, all this is simply knowledge about reality, yet for a "non-believer" this will never be enough. As physicist Paul Davies writes in his book *God and the New Physics,*

> It is hard to resist the impression that the present structure of the universe, apparently so sensitive to minor alterations in the numbers, has been rather carefully thought out. . . . In the end it boils down to a question of belief.

But think about it. Wouldn't that be precisely what God would want, namely for us to make a choice about our spirituality and our knowledge of God? Isn't that the way it should be? Personally, I don't think we'll ever be able to prove the existence of a divine force in evolution or any other spiritual tenet to the complete satisfaction of science. I believe God will give us just enough for "pure faith." God wants followers who choose God out of their spiritual sense and faith, out of what they feel deep in their soul and heart.

We all have this spiritual sense, this pure faith deep within us – whether or not we choose to recognize it is another issue. Two examples of this kind of faith stem from the inhumane circumstances of World War II. In her book *A History of God,* Roman Catholic nun and scholar Karen Armstrong describes how a group of Jews in the Auschwitz concentration camp one day decided to put God on trial. God was brought up on charges of betrayal and cruelty. Since God is supposed to promote universal justice and prevent innocent suffering, arguments for and against God ensued on God's neglect. The rabbi announced the verdict: God was nowhere to be found and guilty as charged. Then the rabbi looked up and declared the trial over; it was time for the evening prayer. Faith was victorious over emotion.

Another example of instinctual, unshaken faith was discovered by Allied soldiers on a basement wall of an abandoned, bombed-out house in Germany at the end of World War II. Scratched into the wall by one of the victims of the Holocaust was the poignant message: "I believe in the sun, even when it does not shine. I believe in love, even when it is not shown. I believe in God, even when [God] does not speak."

This awareness of one's spirituality, this pure faith, is why spiritual pursuits have persisted throughout humankind's history with little if any verifiable evidence of supernatural beings to support it. It is our "knowledge" of God shining through.

### Atheism as a Disease

God never wrought miracles to convince atheism, because [God's] ordinary works convince it.        —Francis Bacon

Against overwhelming logic, some atheists continue to claim that the universe and human life were created by chance.
                    —Quantum chemist Henry Schaefer

Those who are unspiritual do not receive the gifts of God's Spirit, for they are foolishness to them, and they are unable to understand them because they are spiritually discerned.
    —St. Paul in his first letter to the people of Corinth (2:14)

I'm an atheist, thank God.        —Woody Allen

I am becoming more and more convinced that atheism, a choice one makes to deny God and one's spiritual sense, may be one of the most destructive choices of all. A nation full of atheists is downright dangerous.

Don't get me wrong. I'm not saying that atheists have no morals. It's simply that they have less of a *reason* for morals. Morals and ethics do not serve an atheist to the extent or in the manner they serve a person with a growing awareness of God; their values are a function of and relate only to the self and not a higher power. As University of California professor Phillip Johnson says, "If we are accidental products of a purposeless cosmos, as science currently tells us, then there are no objective values which we are obligated to respect. Value is inherently a human creation in a naturalistic universe."

To an atheist, one is the creator of one's own meaning and purpose. There is no ultimate entity to whom one is responsible or accountable. Humankind becomes its own authority, and thus it becomes easier to flee from living responsibly. These assertions reflect the *moral* argument for the existence of God— which states that humankind desires morality and aspires to beatitude. Therefore God is practically and morally necessary (God is the condition of the highest possible good).

The importance of faith and its relation to morals is precisely why, when designing a community organization that would strive to address spiritual issues and solve community problems, I chose to involve only those people who were strong spiritually—those who worked to include God in their everyday lives. These spiritual people have reason to consider values more frequently, and values and good works go together.

Further, I find atheism to be a kind of *dis-ease*—and could certainly make a strong case for "disease" status in that it is dramatically out of the norm and negatively affects quality of life. From connections I've had with the atheists I've known, though I've honestly tried to avoid seeing problems that were not there, I've found them generally to fall into two categories.

The first group of atheists, in my experience, have a deep psychological hurt in which they tend to punish God by denying God. After all, the way to hurt God the most is to deny God's existence—and you don't need to obey an entity that doesn't exist. The other group of atheists, I've found, are arrogant, fallacious thinkers. Sometimes these are scientists, physicians and psychologists who mistake their tools for themselves and buy wholesale into the notion that because they can affect life, they have ultimate control and power over it.

Occasionally I have noted outright hostility among atheists toward those who know God. Many seem angry at spiritually-directed people. Clearly the famous atheist Friedrich Nietzsche attacked religion and, in particular, Christianity and Jesus with such ferocity and contempt that one must question the origin of such vehement passions (he suffered a great deal in his life).

I have yet to find an atheist who can make a compelling argument for atheism. Some atheists suggest believers are fickle—having faith when life goes well but doubting God during hard times. When provided with evidence contradicting that assertion, atheists reverse themselves and say that believers need a crutch to withstand their crises, falling back on God during hard times. Both their hostility and contradictory, illogical arguments often make me wonder what atheists are hiding from.

In all sincerity I feel sorry for them, as I'm sure many do, not just because they often have a lack of meaning and purpose in their lives, but they have never connected with their inner knowledge of God. By denying their spiritual sense, they have never become whole people.

## A Spiritual Paradigm For Living

I should reiterate here that I believe the scientific method is *essential* to society; we unequivocally need science and should promote its progress. But we have lived for so long in a world handicapped by seeing reality in only one way that I have no choice but to be firm in my position that we need a new paradigm for living, one which includes God and the spirit in the entirety of our life.

I remember once when I was getting ready to give a talk on the Schroeder-Lefavi model and the God Theory that a well-respected academician whispered to me, "Just make sure you give both sides." Why? We've been living on only one side for two centuries. If I seem a bit hard on science, it's simply because I'm trying to get on the playing field.

Only our belief in what is real limits our capacity to see all that is there. St. Augustine believed our inner knowledge of God was intelligible (sensed with the mind's eye) and thus a reflection of eternal reality, making it more real than things we perceive with our five senses. Centuries later René Descartes wrote, "I see that there is manifestly more reality in infinite substance than in finite, and therefore that in some way I have in me the notion of the infinite earlier than the finite." How interesting that in our era Stanford professor Willis Harman wrote that a true representation of science is based on two major assumptions:

> an ontological assumption of oneness, wholeness, interconnectedness of everything [notice the concept of universal connection], and an epistemological assumption that we contact reality in not one but two ways. One of these is through physical sense data – which form the basis of normal science. The other is through ourselves being part of the oneness – through a deep "inner knowing."

So, I have come to take an approach to spirituality that can be labelled noetic (encompassing knowledge from many realms). It would be nice to be able to discuss spirituality as a function of pure faith. Certainly, I would make no apologies for doing so. However, in the modern world, I understand all too well that many people need reasons to believe. By recognizing spiritual truths in the world, one's heart can then be opened, one's spiritual sense acknowledged and a process of growth initiated. Each individual, and all people together, could begin to make use of the best of both worlds. In short, both kinds of truth-seekers need each other.

To borrow a concept from Fritjof Capra, *scientists don't need spiritual scholars and spiritual scholars don't need scientists, but humankind needs both!*

# 6

# Our Non-Spiritual World

Although for me the rift between science and spirituality was the chief roadblock in my daily awareness of God, when I spoke with others on similar spiritual journeys, I found that many viewed their *experiences* in the modern world as exacerbating the cognitive dissonance they feel from trying to live with one foot in the world of scientific proof and the other in the world of spiritual awareness. Failure to recognize their spirituality plus the experiences they encounter in society make it easy for them to bury their spiritual sense—to deny God. There are other, often related influences that hinder one's awareness of spirituality and God.

## A Society With a Sick Soul

Any religion which professes to be concerned about the souls of men and is not concerned about the social and economic

conditions that can scar the soul, is a spiritually moribund religion only waiting for the day to be buried.
— Reverend Martin Luther King, Jr.

"If my people, which are called by my name, shall humble themselves, and pray, and seek my face, and turn from their wicked ways; then I will hear from heaven, and will forgive their sin, and will heal their land." — 2 Chronicles 7:14

We often fail to see the detrimental effects society's trends are developing. I see the movement away from spirituality in America paying harmful dividends both personally and socially. This was not the original intent of the nation. John Winthrop and the Puritans aboard the *Arabella* in 1630 saw themselves as chosen people blessed by God whose purpose was to exalt God and live in faith. They considered America the world's last chance at truly communal, spiritual living.

Interestingly, those who followed the Puritans also highly valued the concept of an American *spiritual* community, yet also saw *religious diversity* as good and cited many problems with a national church. However, the essence of many of society's past and present ailments stems from the unfortunate but generally accepted viewpoint that these two initiatives can*not* co-exist, so in order to assure religious freedom, society must also separate itself from any sense of a common spirituality.

## Church and State "Mute"ations and Truths

For most Americans, the relationship between religious belief and scientific understanding is not capable of the neat separation that our legal rhetoric sometimes seems to suppose.
— Yale law professor Stephen L. Carter

The First Amendment's religion clauses were originally an attempt by James Madison, Fisher Ames and Congress (ratified in Bill of Rights, 1791) to ensure that the rights of no person would be abridged due to religious belief or worship and that no national religion would be established, the latter specifically to protect the established churches in seven of the thirteen states as well as to safeguard the powers of the states. This issue became increasingly pertinent and critical since colonial dissenters were tired of being taxed only to see their tax money supporting ministers who were trying to suppress them (most notably the Virginia dissenters), and desperately wanted to guarantee their future religious independence.

Since then, however, the separation of church and state has become a divisive issue in America. Many questions continue to arise in the church-state arguments. First, "accommodationists" (those arguing against a complete, literal separation) claim that the Constitution does not refer to a "separation of church and state." This assertion is true; Jefferson only referred to a "wall of separation" in his 1802 letter to the Danbury Baptists.

Separationists claim this point is mute, that clearly what was meant was a separation. This assertion is also likely to be true. The framers of the Constitution believed both church and state do better when neither one supports or intervenes with the other. Yes, it was a good idea to separate the authority structures that were chiefly responsible for repression of people by many other governments.

The contentious issue here for both sides is determining how permeable this "wall" of separation is. Accommodationists point to Jefferson's recommendation and subsequent signing of a treaty to provide funding for the Kaskaskia Indians to worship in a Catholic church, as well as Presidents Monroe, John Quincy Adams, Jackson and Van Buren's funding to religious organizations in order for Christianity to be taught to Indian tribes as evidence that this "wall" was not meant to be completely impermeable. Once again, true. Similarly, separationists point to numerous Supreme Court decisions solidifying the concept that our Constitution places strict limits on the power of government–both federal and state–to legislate about religion. True as well.

So how permeable *is* this wall? Accommodationists narrowly interpret the First Amendment as stating the idea of separation was not a universal principle applying to the whole of the federal and state system. They do not view this amendment as making illegal many religious actions by both federal and state governments, including benevolently accommodating, protecting and encouraging religious convictions, values and practices. Generally, they see the framers of the Constitution as being "non-preferentialists," who believe the government should be allowed to support religious beliefs and practices so long as it does not *favor* any one religious sect or belief.

On the other hand, separationists interpret the language of the First Amendment differently. They see the wall between church and state as impenetrable; since the Constitution delegates no power to government to establish and control religion. Such lack of power, they feel, implies that government should operate completely outside religion.

I have come to believe *all* of these points are moot. Certainly the legality of these issues is of some importance and what the framers meant is significant at least from an academic viewpoint, but we are no longer dealing with a society like the one existing in the late 18th century. We have a much different society with many diverse and destructive issues requiring management. We are not, at this point, paranoid about the potential damage of religious persecution; rather we are seeing problems associated with a valueless, spiritually devoid society.

What is meaningful in today's vastly different society is not understanding what the framers of the Constitution "meant" or what was important then, but what "is" now! Second, another reason the church-state issue is moot is because the separation of church and state refers to the separation of state and religion, not spirituality. The recognition of a higher power and the importance of spirituality to the individual have been around long before the establishment of religious organizations.

When most people think of church-state issues, they think of prayer in school. Yes, it's illegal for the state to organize, support or require school prayer. We should all be concerned about the government regulating religiosity. However, while prayer is considered a religious practice by many, clearly prayer is foremost a spiritual practice – one that recognizes something greater than ourselves as having importance and value in our lives. If I had to make a good case for a prayer time in schools, I could; rather I choose to suggest a moment of silence in which students can opt to recognize and briefly reconnect to the spiritual part of themselves.

Third, it should be noted that current church-state issues go much further than just prayers in school. How permeable this wall is remains a personal decision, but it certainly appears flimsy. Consider the other ways church and state interact: business closing regulations on Sunday, religiosity and politics, abortion, tax exemption for religious institutions, to name a few. I have witnessed public fire departments putting out church fires and invocations by clergy at public school commencements. So this separation is not total; there are many holes in the metaphoric wall. I do not believe completely in the separation of church and state because I don't believe it is completely possible.

Finally, although church and state function better when they don't support or intervene with each other, this does not mean they ought to be *indifferent* to one another or fail to recognize how they may indirectly interact. National recognition of common interests, especially when no person is significantly affected adversely, is good.

Why *should* we change? Because of the damage that is created both personally and socially if we don't. But we've heard all that before, right? So what's different now?

What's different now, without sounding too much like a politician or a preacher, is that social and personal damage truly *has* reached epidemic proportions. We really *do appear* to have many crises on our hands, especially with America's young people. How much worse off our social problems can get is unknown–and frightening.

In the first half of this century, the national illegitimacy rate was about five percent, now it is over 30 percent while in some neighborhoods of large cities the figure is in the 80s. Nationally, according to demographers, we are expected to have an *average* illegitimacy rate of 40 percent (including all areas) by the end of the century. In 1970, there were 2.1 million marriages in this country with 700,00 divorces–a ratio of one divorce for every three marriages. In 1995, there were 2.3 million marriages and 1.2 million divorces–a ratio of about one divorce for every two marriages.

Of families headed by a woman with no husband present in 1995, just under 40 percent lived in poverty. This is critical as one considers that the number of single mothers in the U.S. jumped about 60 percent between 1980 and 1997, from 6.3 million to 10.0 million. A 1996 Department of Health and Human Services report on teenage drug use (12-17 yrs.) found that drug use had increased 78 percent between 1992 and 1995. Specifically, the use of cocaine increased 166 percent, hallucinogens (LSD, etc.) went up 54 percent and marijuana rose 37 percent! Between 1950 and 1992, suicide among adolescents and young adults nearly tripled according to the Centers for Disease Control and Prevention. Likewise, in a 1993 Youth at Risk Survey in which 16,000 high school students participated, nearly a quarter of these students stated they had seriously considered attempting suicide the previous year!

Is this just a function of normal adolescent conflicts? No, at least it's not normal everywhere. Case in point is Victor Frankl's work in which he ascertained that 20 percent of Austrian students feel a sense of meaninglessness while 60 percent of students in America feel a lack of meaning in their lives. When you begin to look at what will happen if the present rates of teenage pregnancy, nuclear family reduction, drug use and suicide continue, the numbers are sobering and chilling.

In a recent interview, James Q. Wilson, social philosopher at UCLA, explained that the social problems of the Western culture stem from the 18th-century Enlightenment movement:

> We put in place in this country political institutions designed to have a limited government, a government that would play no role in character formation, a government that would be separated from the church, and a government constrained by an elaborate Bill of Rights....People want to come to this country desperately because of the advantages. We have the most prosperous economy in the world. But also the costs grew up faster, these dank weeds in the Enlightenment garden grew up here, in this country, better than they grew up in Sweden or Scotland or other nations that had a more established order....So we have the best of the best and the worst of the worst.

This, Wilson believes, has come home to roost in the latter half of the 20th century.

### The Lowest Common Denominator

> If God did not exist, everything would be permitted.
> —Dostoyevsky

Upon encountering the data on a variety of our social dilemmas I have a habit of asking, "What is the root cause?" That is, even considering the many factors influencing personal decisions, it is prudent to ask, "What one factor, if any, could this problem be traced to for most people?" Sure, you might find poor choices and strokes of bad luck, but too often what I find is that real values and morals are missing.

Simply put, American society no longer has the *spiritual glue* that keeps any well-functioning society together. When you look deeply into the underlying situation in which amoral behavior takes root, the lowest common denominator is frequently a disconnection from and a lack of awareness of one's spirituality and relationship with God. This pervasive dearth of spiritual living has facilitated a society in which price tags could be switched. As we promote sports champions and actors as culture heroes and as sleazy talk shows unfairly represent the way most Americans live, we have further down-regulated our concept of right and up-regulated our concept of wrong. A denial of the spirit becomes reinforced.

Stephen Carter, in his recent book *The Culture of Disbelief*, blames cultural decay on a growing exclusion of spirituality from public life. "We have pressed the religiously faithful . . . to act as though their faith does not matter," Carter argues. I find it ironic that in class I can talk about the many medical ways to treat drug use, but I must be careful if I discuss the overwhelming body of literature showing religiosity to be inversely related to all types of drug abuse. Go figure.

I am convinced that part of the solution to these social problems resides in our recognition of a higher power, our personal and societal awareness of God in our lives. People are yearning for a new moral order, a new social order. This can come only from a resurgence of spirituality.

"You are our God!...We are helpless in the face of this large army that is attacking us. We do not know what to do, but we look to you for help."                    −2 Chronicles 20:12

Although the national motto may be "In God We Trust," good citizens of the modernist state trust in God only with respect to matters that concern no one but themselves and their families. When they take actions that affect others, trust in God becomes unconstitutional.
                                                          −Law professor Phillip Johnson

Before it can work with anyone else, you have to find peace with yourself....We have to be prepared spiritually in order to try to stop the violence. If we don't have that, it is very easy to get lost in the daily madness and pain.
       −Aaron Gallegos on *Barrios Unidos* against gang violence

Millions of people in this country recite a pledge daily that includes the phrase "one nation under God." But can we truly ever have one nation under God? If not, what must we do to return at least to a balanced America, one which fosters spiritual awareness and growth?

No, I am not about to launch into a Bible-thumping tirade, spewing forth my answer to the country's problems−a return to Biblical morals and a religious society. Rather, I will point to a compromise that allows *values* and *freedom*, two things Americans cherish. By giving credence to our spiritual sense, this compromise will further help us reduce the cognitive dissonance associated with one's spiritual awareness in the modern world. It will help encourage spiritual growth and social responsibility.

First, however, we must look at whether or not fundamental morals and values actually do exist. That is, we clearly live in a society based more on *relative morality* than on absolute moral truths. Is the concept that fundamental, basic moral truths exist in humans valid? For example, even if Moses never told the children of Israel "Thou shalt not kill" and if there were no current law against it, would we still feel it is wrong to kill? I am convinced the answer to this is yes. I am stating, then, that moral law transcends the individual and society. When we agree it is right to promote good and wrong to promote that which is evil, we are at a reasonable starting point.

My compromise, then, is for us all to agree on basic "shared American values." This would in no way be a reigning faith, but rather shared American values would stand as a common core and moral ground in a pluralistic, spiritually aware society. Shared American values would be a set of principles that primarily seeks one outcome – goodness, love and peace; secondarily, it would strive to find the minimum of morality that must be present, shared and observed in any society for it to maintain social stability.

Yes, "values" is a polarizing word. On hearing it, some people immediately become enthusiastic while others might become anxious and guarded and even ask the question, "Isn't this the same as saying we're all going to agree on religious issues, making it a church-state problem?" The answer is no. Besides pointing to the clear distinction between spirituality and religion, I would argue that we cannot have a totally secular society in America; even the Declaration of Independence and the Constitution were based upon certain moral truths. Other societies that tried to limit "religion" to extremes were national socialism in Germany and communism in the Soviet empire.

I firmly believe that by trying we can get to shared American values. Critics might denounce this as being a well-veiled attempt at getting religious principles taught in school. Not true! But schools should be involved in the discussion of shared values. This would foster in children the idea that our society (not just the law) values something greater than ourselves and, as one society, we strive to grow toward an ultimate good.

The best argument to have values *not* discussed in schools is that they should be discussed at home. But they're *not* being discussed. More than half the children in this country are growing up with only a mother or a father as guardian. Further, even when a single parent attempts to educate on values, they often don't have enough time to do a good job in their hectic, one-parent schedule. These two problems are something our founders *never* counted on. They assumed the *family*, being the most important character-building institution and the seedbed of virtue, would remain intact. They were wrong.

As a professor working with thousands of young men and women, I have witnessed the effects on those growing up in a family where God is given "myth" (which children interpret as "unreal") status. I suppose this is why I see that one of my most important jobs as a parent is to help my children understand the relationship they already have with God. What a blessing that my wife feels the same way and what joy there will be at the end of my life when I see how that relationship with God has manifested in my children.

I'm not alone in the realization that we, as a society (not just in our families), need to address spiritual and moral concerns. In a 1996 Gallup poll of over 1,000 American adults, 60 percent said they think the federal government should be involved in promoting moral values in our society. Let's face it, we will probably never go back to the values of early America, but we can make society better through tough decisions and shared values. The great psychologist Abraham Maslow wrote, "We need a validated, usable system of human values that we can believe in and devote ourselves to."

I am convinced that a society that purposely avoids and denies God has an illness that is terminal. A shared set of

American values can help restore the spiritual and moral health of our nation. Moreover, I believe that shared American values means the nation can once again have a vision.

## Pseudo-spirituality

Making matters more confusing for those people who do seek to follow and nurture their spiritual sense in spite of the global denial of spirituality is what they eventually encounter as "spiritual." Just about anything–no matter how totally secular and material its focus–passes for spirituality these days. While searching for truth and purpose, many people become targets for peddlers of what I call "pseudo-spirituality" (false spirituality). Those promoting what, to me, is clearly unauthentic and phoney spirituality seem to be much more interested in getting on the television talk-show circuit than in promoting that which has its basis in age-old spiritual wisdom. Although anyone who helps people live more spiritually can't be all bad, I will focus on how some pseudo-spiritualists seem to miss the point of spirituality.

Here are some examples of what people wishing to grow spiritually might encounter–but what I think would likely turn them off to spirituality in general:

- **Deepak Chopra, MD,** is a spirituality "guru" who seems to enjoy promoting himself as the "Lord of Immortality." In one charismatic piece of writing he explains that when we incorporate the knowledge of morality and the process of divinity in motion (the physical laws of the universe) into our consciousness, we have the ability to create unlimited *wealth* with effortless ease and to experience success in every endeavor. Another book of his focuses on using spiritual truths as a way to live longer–as if living longer is the purpose of life.

  Chopra does not appear to want people asking about his beliefs, how they seem self-serving and conflict with longstanding spiritual wisdom. "Chopra prefers gullible people. They have made him rich," writes Zina Moukheiber in a *Forbes* magazine article. Chopra himself says in a *Newsweek* interview, "I satisfy a spiritual yearning without making [people] think they have to worry about God and punishment."

What kind of spirituality is that? A kind that will sell in an if-it-feels-good-do-it society? Maybe. One that is in accord with spiritual tenets? I don't think so.

• **Wayne Dyer, MD,** follows in Chopra's footsteps in his book *Real Magic.* Like Chopra, Dyer describes how a renewed spirituality can help you attain anything you want, any amount of wealth or material goods. Within pages of citing the importance of Paramhansa Yogananda's words that "it is spiritual poverty, not material lack, that lies at the core of all human suffering," Dyer writes that "as you move along the spiritual path and begin to get a taste of the power of your invisible self, you discover that money-making is merely a game that you play with yourself."

Great, but why does he assume that everyone's purpose (a true subdimension of spirituality) is going to be consistent with material wealth and prosperity? What if your purpose is to be in Calcutta helping the ill? What about helping people by working in social services for just enough to pay the bills? What's more important, purpose or prosperity?

• In **Neale Donald Walsch**'s series of books called *Conversations With God,* Walsch claims that God grabbed his hand one day and started writing answers to his questions. Let me say that spiritual experiences do occur and I believe God does communicate, in God's way, with us. However, it is the content of the coffee-table wisdom emanating from what I see as a series of inane, naïve books that concerns me; it likely would turn those seeking reconnection with God away from their spiritual sense.

For instance, God tells Walsch, "You [referring to humans] are the Highest Source." God, Walsch suggests, also encourages doing what feels good (choosing power, fame, success, and so on) because that validates who you are. Wonderful, but what if it feels good to hurt someone? Is that okay?

Moreover, Walsch explains that God altered God's essence and message—the way God speaks through Walsch—so that Walsch could understand. That would be a new one for God. In every other recorded instance in which God appears to have communicated with humankind, God has been unchanging and has sent God's message God's way; God has never shown a need to "dumb down" communication with us so we would "get it." Further, the drivel God supposedly has spoken is also inconsistent with scripture. As the prophet Jeremiah has written, "Is not my word like a fire? saith the Lord; and like a hammer that breaketh the rock in pieces?" (Jer 23:29). God's communication with us is profound, sometimes not immediately clear to us, but always profound. That Walsch identifies God as channeling through him, using the kind of slang and superficiality Walsch suggests God used, is generally not appreciated by those promoting spiritual growth through the study of God's Word.

It saddens me to think how many people would have a completely wrong idea about spirituality and God by reading this book, one which has been on many bestseller lists. Perhaps its moderate success speaks to what people, in their desire to reconnect with their spiritual sense and God, are willing to accept as spiritual in the modern world.

• In **Paul Zane Pilzer**'s popular book *God Wants You to Be Rich*, Pilzer explains how and why God wants each of us to be materially rich. As might be expected, this book has sold abundantly to people wanting to reduce the cognitive dissonance they feel between their greed and knowledge of longstanding, scripturally consistent spiritual direction; it offers exactly what people want to hear!

I believe God wants us to be part of a master plan and grow spiritually. This might include many possessions for some and not so many for others. Pilzer, of course, has difficulty trying to rationalize why his ideas are inconsistent with scripture (and scripture clearly sends a message that we should not live for worldly goods and selfishness ends). I believe this book to be a beautifully written masterpiece of distorted logic. It might be other things, but for me it has nothing to do with God or one's spirituality.

• What some writers call "the wisdom movement" is based upon a spiritual search, but focuses more on "what's important in life" than on getting in touch with God, which I see as a sort of an oxymoronic purpose. In *What Really Matters,* author **Tony Schwartz** explains that wisdom is the "true" self an inner search uncovers. For Schwartz, it is the "search" itself that counts, not necessarily what one finds. One gets the distinct impression from this book that as long as one goes through an inner search, whatever you find is okay.

Schwartz writes, "It's not truth in some absolute sense that I'm after.... What I'm most committed to is searching for my own truth." I have spoken to many criminals who acted on and were convinced of their own truth.

• Any television evangelist who makes a habit of asking for money from viewers. Your spiritual growth, and indeed spirituality itself, is free. These evangelists send a message that spirituality is quid pro quo. If people want to support them because they enjoy their programs, fine. However, we should not confuse the evangelists, many of whom beg for your money while wearing $2,500 suits and living in luxury, with that which represents an awareness of God – one's true spirituality.

## Commerce With Conscience

Fortunately, not all encounters with the promotion of spirituality in society are as ill-founded. The movement toward a spiritual renewal in the workplace incorporates more positive than negative influences; it seems to be both well-intentioned and effective, though some of it remains greed-oriented.

Some companies turn inward in search of their "soul." This movement is an attempt to create a sense of meaning and purpose at work and foster a connection between the company and its employees. Companies are hoping that the combination of head and heart will create an advantage. As Scott Cook, founder of Intuit which makes Quicken software, has said, "What I've learned . . . is that being truthful is good business. You may solve some temporary bind by fibbing, but it will come back to haunt you. It's not just wrong; it also doesn't work."

Clearly, where there is money, there is often greed, yet I suppose I am a bit less opposed to spirituality being peddled to enhance business. At least, one might suggest, it is not completely self-serving to be able to keep many others employed. This effort is also in line with the teaching of Gandhi – one of his seven sins was "commerce without conscience." I look forward to more ideas on how authority and power can be used with love in business and how one can recognize where employees are, spiritually.

*Spirituality As A Tool*

As more people than ever move into middle-age in America, questions of meaning and purpose and a recognition of one's spiritual sense bring many to seek avenues of spiritual growth. I am concerned that marketers see this as an opportunity to promote spirituality in a strictly secular sense – as a new chic, giving rise to anything-goes, ill-founded "wisdom." However, for one truly to grow in spirit, one's spirituality must resonate deeply within the soul – at a person's core. Like Jesus' parable of the sower of seeds, when true wisdom falls on stony, shallow ground, it rises up too quickly and withers away as soon as the sun hits it because it has no deep roots.

Pseudo-spirituality can be damaging largely because of the message it sends – that spirituality can or should be used as a "means to another end" (to become wealthy, to ward off aging, to find your true self, etc.). Chopra, in particular, focuses on good health, giving the impression in his writings that health is the "end" desired. The aims of his books on spirituality and health appear to be about living longer and being more healthy, but what does this have to do with spirituality? It's great to be healthy, but as medical researcher Rachel Naomi Remen says, "Health enables us to serve purpose in our life, but it is not the purpose in life. One can serve purpose with impaired health. One might even regain health through serving purpose."

Health is a *means* to an end, not an end in itself. Spirituality shouldn't be used for some other purpose; it is our highest purpose. As Larry Dossey writes in *Healing Words,* "To use spirituality for a specific purpose would be a contradiction in terms, an exercise in hypocrisy." Let's not make spirituality just another self-help method.

In addition, spirituality has often been used as a tool for vindication and persecution. Of those who saw him, few can forget the sight of O.J. Simpson in church with a Bible saying, "I have God on my side." Further, the fact is that every country that has ever gone to war believed they had God on their side. These people are confused about God and spirituality and, unfortunately, they turn many others away from spiritual pursuits.

Finally, the cited examples of pseudo-spirituality suggest that one's spirituality should be used for *our* glory. I have yet to see any spiritual tenet or scripture in any major religion or related spiritually-based organization that is consistent with that suggestion. Rather, spiritual wisdom across the globe tells us that we are here, in part, to carry out God's will, love one another, grow in spirit and glorify *God.*

In all this we must avoid throwing out the proverbial baby with the bath water. Spiritual truths are what they are–unchanging–and no amount of false wisdom or slick marketing can alter them. Don't let the pseudo-spirituality of others hinder your spiritual awareness and growth.

## Life's Not Fair

Another aspect of our experiences in society that turns some away from their spiritual pursuits is the inconsistency people see between life's tragedies and the concept of a higher power directing the universe. One look at the evening news will leave anyone questioning whether divine justice can possibly exist. We see racial, legal and national injustices daily. How could God allow all that to occur?

Specifically, this is the "theodicy" (*Theos* and *dice* being Greek for God and justice, respectively) question of divine justice, a dilemma pondered by philosophers and theologians for millennia. Think of it as trying to reconcile three points in a triangle, namely (a) an all-powerful, omnipotent God, (b) a benevolent God who desires good to exist, and (c) apparently innocent suffering. If all three of these exist, the dilemma dictates, then something is terribly wrong; they just don't fit together. A God who can do anything and wants good to occur would not allow apparently innocent suffering.

In an increasingly violent, seemingly unfair world, while searching for the point that ties them all together, some people will naturally become frustrated and assume it is the omnipotent, benevolent deity that doesn't fit. When nothing makes sense, they will presume there can be no higher power. More dissonance takes place and God along with their spirituality gets buried even deeper.

In my spiritual journey, I've facilitated groups on crises and tragedies from divorce to homicide; if I've haven't heard it all, I've heard most of it! From angry people asking, "Why doesn't God just fix this?" to those deep in depression saying, "I still believe in God, I just want to know where God's been!"

*Divine Guidance?*

While in no way do I claim to have more insight into the theodicy dilemma than anyone else, let me note two things: First, in many situations it's difficult to see exactly what God does and exactly what humankind does. Second, scripture in the vast array of spiritual teachings around the world supports a perfect master plan. Although not all that happens in the plan is *in itself* good, taken all together, scripture describes events as working for the greater good of God's plan. I know, that's little consolation when it's you on the short end of the stick.

I suppose I have come to see the theodicy dilemma as a sort of Rubik's Cube. That is, I believe that God took a perfect plan, where everything was connected, fit together as it should (only one way), and spread it all out during the Big Bang. At that moment, time started and God began working to bring the universe all back to God's perfect plan. Like a Rubik's Cube, when you just look at any two pieces (events), they may not seem to belong or make sense next to each other. However, by looking at the whole, which is only possible when it's completed, the sides go together perfectly; in fact, they *have* to fit together that way. Perhaps that is a function of one's spiritual sense – the inner knowledge that God knows the master plan and the trust that, if we ask, *God will guide us* in the playing of our part.

So in the theodicy dilemma we see how our experiences in the modern world may exacerbate the cognitive dissonance and confusion we feel when we consider a God who's involved in our lives. Thus, the theodicy question provides more fuel to the denial of God and one's spirituality, particularly in a world that has difficulty seeing past its immediate context.

## Religious Limitations

Before researching and understanding the differences between spirituality and religion, I considered spirituality to be defined by my religion. Clearly, religious institutions are not the only ways to spiritually grow with God. Only as I began to see the limitations of organized religion did its potential negative effects on spirituality become apparent

The divisiveness, compartmentalization and separation of

"our" religion from "their" religion detract from the purpose of religion as being a means of growing spiritually in peace and harmony. To be sure, being proud of and loyal to your religion is commendable, but when we adhere more to the organization itself than to the universal message it brings us, it becomes confining.

Once when I was speaking, a minister stood up and started his sentence with "We Baptists don't usually believe in what you said . . ." while another minister approached me to say, "Your man Billy Graham . . ." We must be careful within religious organizations to avoid becoming non-thinking sheep. It is too easy for that to occur and for diversity to give way to divisiveness; hatred and fear–masked as rules and fundamentalist beliefs–can bring people ever further from the underlying truths of spiritual tenets.

When we bring dogmatism into our spiritual lives, we lose sight of tolerance and mystery as spiritual truths. Specifically, by aligning oneself too closely with the human-made dogma of organized religion, we have a tendency to view other religions as threats to our beliefs; we believe their final word is that they want us to be like them. Rather, a spiritually whole person embraces any religion that strives to foster growth of the spirit, goodness, mutual acceptance and respect and universal, unconditional love.

Making matters worse, many people turn on their televisions to see the destructive nature of religious cults. Again, this is not spirituality. A growing spirituality encourages you to open up and embrace others, to become involved in your community. Cults demand that you close yourself off from others, often including your family. Seeing "religion" tied to cults hurts our perception of the importance of following our spiritual sense.

We must come together in spirituality, not religion. "The problem is how to translate many disparate religious experiences into a coherent worldview," says physicist Paul Davies. True, but it can be done. How? By learning about other religions. It is only then that we see how similar they really are. When we know only one religion, answers are easy; we simply take the point of view presented by that religion. But when we know many religions, answers are more complex and mysterious, but also more liberating and exciting.

Also, when we study and delve into other religions, we see that the major religions have much more in common than they have differences. Clearly, there *are* differences, but to learn, and to seek harmony and tolerance among the religions is enlightening and a superb path to the essence of spirituality – a love of God and others.

## Common Ground

When we become familiarized with the various religions, we can move from religious problems to spiritual truths. Distilling the great religions down to their basic tenets and wisdom, we often find differences to be few. The principles of most major religions are consistent with one another. There are spiritual truths in and some harmony among all the world's great religions.

For instance, they all point to the "divine" as that which does not depend on anything else for its existence and which has a plan for the reign of goodness. They extol a vision of a grand design that is better and more mysterious than it seems. They present the Golden Rule as a key aspect of community and love and describe the importance of creed and deed – holding humility, charity, tolerance and veracity as important virtues, while murder, theft, dishonesty and adultery are pro-scribed. Even Islam, a little understood religion in the West, does this.

The spiritual truths in all religions may be difficult to see from each individual's vantage point. Wading through dogma and scripture can be arduous, and interpretations are far from perfect because scripture was written and interpreted by humans. The point is that as we grow spiritually, each religion we explore can keep its own integrity. We simply begin to appreciate the spiritual truths each one brings. In his book *The Search for God at Harvard,* Ari Goldman describes how he found the true spirituality of his own religion while learning about others and seeking harmony. Religion is not really limiting at all if we focus on the spiritual truths within each expression.

What is revealing to me is how different the major religions *could* and *would* be if they were completely independent – *if they were not describing the same things.* I like to think of major religions as being different software used to connect to a mainframe computer (God), with every religion believing that only theirs works. With so many opportunities for interfaith studies on the spiritual truths and the harmony between the major religions, it's disheartening that religious organizations and their often rigid compartmentalizing dogma have kept many persons from opening up to and exploring their spirituality.

## Death and Life

The unexamined death is not worth dying.
— Robert Kavanaugh in *Facing Death*

When we confront death, our spirituality becomes momentarily unavoidable. Even then, however, many let that opportunity to reconnect to their spiritual sense pass because death itself is a part of the spiritual denial we experience in society.

I'll never forget the day I was moments from going on the air as guest on a cable television talk show–the topic of which was death and dying. The host turned to me and said, "Now let's keep this upbeat. We don't want to lose any viewers, O.K.?" To me this was the epitome of our society's reaction to the entire subject of death. We don't really want to think about death, much less talk about it, and if we must discuss death, then we'll at least try to avoid anything gloomy. We develop euphemisms for dying and say a relative "passed away" or that we "lost" someone. I believe these are just reflections of our desire to evade the reality and permanence of physical death. But such avoidance hinders a key step in our spiritual growth.

Death is the last American taboo, the most unpopular of topics. When was the last time you had a conversation about other "forbidden" topics–such as sex, religion, or politics? Probably not long ago. When was the last time you sat down with someone to discuss any aspect of death? See what I mean?

Why bother thinking about it anyway, right? After all, it's depressing and probably not the most polite dinner conversation. Sure, this reasoning works fine, until someone we know dies and we're blindsided and dumbfounded, not having come to grips with the inevitability and sheer reality of death. By not dealing with death openly and actively we (a) are less prepared when someone close to us dies, and (b) compromise our ability to reach our *full potential of spiritual growth* (remember, a sub-dimension of spirituality is belief in an afterlife).

## Mindful Living

I am absolutely convinced that our reluctance to think about and discuss death is not as much an attempt to avoid what many people view as a depressing matter as it is a function of our society's *widespread denial of death, a tactic that parallels the denial of our spirituality.* We have a tendency to eliminate the issue of death, particularly our own death, from our consciousness and by removing it from our everyday mindfulness, we exclude it from our daily life.

The irony of this is two-fold: First, most people eliminate from their consciousness the only thing in life they can truly count on. Second, one of the few things that separates us as human beings from other species is our capacity to grasp the concept of a future – and inevitable – death. Yet, we have a penchant for skirting the issue purposefully.

I'm not saying we don't believe we'll die. Of course, we do. (Even those of us who exercise hard and eat right will eventually die of something. As the great philosopher Red Foxx once said, "All those health nuts will feel pretty stupid one day when they're lying on their death bed, dying of nothing!") Rather, what I am suggesting is that we bury the issue of death and deny the true reality of death at our most conscious level – the *mindfulness of our daily living.*

Making matters worse, the more that scientific technology advances, the more we are able to avoid the conscious reality of death. We are convinced medicine will come up with a cure for everything soon. Likewise, death has become so mechanized, lonely and dehumanized that we are easily able to separate its reality from our everyday life.

In our unconscious, we can't perceive our own death and do not believe in our mortality. In her consequential book *On Death and Dying,* Elisabeth Kubler-Ross writes, "Man is not freely willing to look at his own end of life on earth and will only occasionally and halfheartedly take a glimpse at the possibility of his own death."

*Fear as the Great Paralyzer.* Why do we avoid death as a

topic to be discussed like any other and fail to live mindful of our life's transitory nature? I think it is because we fear death.

I have seen people go to extraordinary lengths at great expense to look much younger than they are. Likewise, I've observed others hoarding and collecting as much money and big-kid toys as they possibly can. It seems to me that for some of them, growing older is a reminder they are closer to death and since death elicits such great fear, they respond by trying to "turn back the clock" (as if a tighter face, younger girlfriend or a ton of money can protect them from the inevitable).

The fear of death, whether stemming from a fear of suffering or of the unknown, paralyzes some. It's as if they quit taking risks, learning and growing. Often, so much effort is put into trying to minimize their death anxiety these people actually stop enjoying life. In fact, some psychologists believe that this death anxiety is at the core of all human fears.

Paralyzing anxiety about death can manifest itself at any age, though it often takes hold following the death of a loved one. I believe this is why so many books about death have become bestsellers lately. The 80 million Baby Boomers in this country—now between about 34 and 52 years of age—are, by and large, just beginning to experience the deaths of their parents, uncles and aunts. Since this group is currently driving the American marketplace, it's no wonder that books about how we die and what happens to us when we die (death anxiety issues) are being written and have become so popular.

*The Paradox of Death*

Besides reducing fear and increasing mindfulness, discussing death openly and actively helps us come to grips with our mortality. When we accept our mortality and see that we have a limited amount of time to make a difference, we take risks, have fun, strive to live fully each day and *become spiritually aware and alive!* Thus, the paradox of death is that *by accepting death, we can find our life.* As the ancient Greek philosopher Epicurus said, "Where life is, death is not."

> Acceptance of personal mortality is one of the foremost entryways to self-knowledge. Human maturity brings along with it a recognition of limit....In emphasizing awareness of death, we sharpen and intensify our appreciation of the uniqueness and preciousness of life. In responding to our temporality, we shall find it easier to define values, priorities, and life goals.

So wrote psychologist Herman Fiefel. Reflecting this paradox, Victor Frankl, a few years before he died said,

> We do an injustice to death by believing that it deprives and robs life of meaning. Actually, it doesn't take the meaning away from but rather gives meaning to life. Imagine what would happen if our lives were not finite, if we were immortal....Only under the threat and pressure of death does it make sense to do what we can and should, right now.

In those brief moments of mindfulness and clarity, when confronted with our own mortality, we find life's deepest questions and most precious answers.

*Wall or Door?* Does death represent a wall or a door to you? Your answer determines your ability to live fully the life you have been given, reaching your potential of mind, body and spirit. We have seen this freedom from the fear of death acutely in those who have near-death experiences and subsequently live their life completely differently – happier than they had ever imagined – with a basic shift in consciousness whereby life in every moment becomes vivid and free.

In support groups for grieving families, I have noticed that when people describe the death of a young person, they express extreme sadness because a life has been shortened. Their actions and words are remembered differently, as if the entirety of a life was framed by death. It is believed that young people have died prematurely without having had the chance to live. Likewise, when speaking with those who are dying, I have found that some wish they had a few more years disease-free so they could do all the things they now realize are so important.

Yet all of our lives are short and framed by death. We *all* have a deadline. In the grand scheme of the universe, 25 years is not that much different from 75. So how many of us really live mindful of the preciousness of every conversation, every prayer, every moment? Not many. At the time of our death, it is likely that we, like those who I've spoken to prior to their death, will look at our life as a few years too short. We might never have gotten around to living fully awake.

*A Dynamite Story.* Few people know the story of Alfred Nobel, the inventor of dynamite. Nobel spent his very successful life accumulating a fortune through the invention, production and sale of weapons. One morning in 1888 Nobel awoke to read his obituary in the paper! In fact, a French journalist had confused Nobel with his brother and reported the demise of Alfred instead. Alfred read how the world would remember him—"the dynamite king" who became rich by inventing things that destroyed. He realized the public would view this as the sum of his life. As he read his obituary, Nobel was horrified and resolved the world would remember him differently; they would be clear as to the true purpose of his life.

In his last will and testament, Nobel described his life's ideals, emphasizing his desire to break down barriers between people and ideas. He left his fortune to be distributed as a Nobel prize given to those who have done the most for the cause of world peace. Nobel had the opportunity to awaken to his death – and thus to his life, purpose and spiritual sense.

The fear and denial of death helps us avoid thinking about the afterlife (and life itself), keeps us from giving credence to our spiritual sense and from living mindfully and abundantly. This is another aspect of our experiences in the modern world that *promotes our estrangement from God and our spirituality.*

## Re-"Yin"-ification

For trusteth wel, it is an impossible
That any clerk wol speke good of wyves,
But if it be of hooly seinted lyves . . .
By God! If wommen hadde writen stories,
As clerkes han withinne hire oratories,
They wolde han writen of men moore wikkednesse
Than al the mark of Adam may redresse . . .
— Chaucer, *The Wife of Bath's Prologue*

The modern world keeps many from spiritual awareness in yet another way. I have found that when we begin to listen to our spiritual sense, when we open up and travel down the difficult path of introspection and change, we become *softer.* A spiritual person is a more gentle, tolerant and caring soul.

Unfortunately, little in our society promotes compassion and softness; we are too busy "yang"ing around. Our world is male-dominated and as such, is focused on competitiveness, aggression and conquest. Virtually every world system that influences others is based upon power and dominance, characteristics that oppose spiritual tenets. Even the common terminology we use is male-oriented. In commerce, besides there being an abundance of hostility and competitiveness, we often describe "take-overs" and companies hurting each other. In the health sciences talk of the immune system "attacking" this and "killing" that is routine (though that's not the way the immune system works;

it needs to be balanced, not strengthened).

This male-dominated orientation, I believe, may keep some men, and possibly even some women, from exploring their spirituality as they begin to feel a desire to "soften," to be more tolerant and compassionate. In other words, in the case of a man seeking spiritual fulfillment, as he becomes more balanced, taking on some "yin" qualities the world associates with women (for example, he may lose his taste for ego-boosting achievement, and so on), he might feel dissonance and conflict created by what the world expects, encourages and rewards, and defer to it as it offers tangible rewards.

In short, we must give credence to both the "yin" and the "yang." I believe that a *complete, spiritually aware person needs both;* thus our society needs both. There must be a place for love, compassion and benevolence – the essence of God and our spiritual sense – in the fabric of the modern world.

## Healing The Schizophrenia

Many practicing scientists are also religious. Following the publication of *God and the New Physics,* I was astonished to discover how many of my close scientific colleagues practice a conventional religion. In some cases they manage to keep these two aspects of their lives separate, as if science rules six days a week and religion on Sunday. – Physicist Paul Davies

The secret of my success? It is simple. It is found in the Bible, "In all thy ways acknowledge God and God shall direct thy paths." George Washington Carver

Not wanting to lose their faith nor to reject the truth yielded by science and experience, many have found a refuge by living in two worlds at different times of the day, not unlike the schizophrenic. – Scientist David Snoke

After finding reasons to believe, my journey of spiritual awareness confirmed that it's becoming increasingly difficult to be a spiritual person in the modern world. It appears we have no choice but to lead two lives. For many, these two separate existences take the form of living one day a week under a spiritual reality, then entering the "real" world and its reality on Monday. We must recognize how the systematic elimination of God and our spirituality from the everyday world dramatically hinders our potential to grow spiritually.

Fortunately, a lot of educated people are refusing to make this destructive separation in their lives. Even many scientists don't believe they have to check their brains at the door when they enter church, synagogue or mosque. When I got back in touch with the knowledge of the divine that was inside of me, *that there is a benevolent, loving God was the only thing I knew clearly.* I saw everything else as the shadow world; the material world and science were quickly relegated to a back seat. It took a while for me to get beyond the dissonance and the denial of God I had accepted from the modern world for so long.

### Spirit "Matters"

The culmination of my journey was the discovery of *harmony and reconciliation between matter and spirit.* This allowed me to overcome the denial of God and my spirituality, enabling me to see reality through eyes of the spirit and truth. Again, my purpose in showing the consistency between science and spirituality is not to put God under the microscope (remember, the supernatural is not constrained by natural laws, we can only measure its effects), but rather to assist in breaking down the cognitive dissonance many people feel about spiritual truths in today's world, confusion which results in the relegation of God and their spirituality to myth. If it takes "reasons to believe" to foster spiritual awareness in modern society, as it did for me, then so be it.

*An Deus sit?*

Do I, or does anyone, have all the answers for those who *are* aware of their spiritual sense and are searching for true spirituality and personal growth? No, but the questions are becoming clearer. For instance, perhaps the question most asked in all of humankind's history, that which Thomas Aquinas asked as he began his famous *Summa Theologiae, "An Deus sit?"* ("Does God exist?") is no longer the appropriate question. Today's question should be "*Can* God exist in the modern world?"

We must answer yes if we are to grow as spiritual people. The next millennium will be one in which leaders in science, society and spirituality work together to solve the world's problems – or it may not be at all. We all must share the understanding that our pervasive spiritual denial means we have no sense of a personal relationship with the Creator, and no sense that our neighbor is our responsibility. Only by awakening our spiritual sense can we ignite that spark of the divine within us, know God's love for us, love God and become spiritually whole people, working together for the good of humankind.

# Notes

## Chapter 1

For more information on Benson's concepts about the biology of belief, see: Benson, H., *Timeless Healing*. NY: Scribner, 1996.

To learn more about noetics, contact the Institute of Noetic Sciences, 475 Gate Five Rd., Ste. 300, P.O. Box 909, Sausalito, CA 94966.

M. Scott Peck's *Road Less Traveled*. NY: Simon & Schuster, 1976.

Fowler's stages of faith are described in: Fowler, J.W., *Stages of Faith*. San Francisco: Harper Row, 1981.

Peck's model of spiritual growth is found in: Peck, M.S., *The Different Drum*. NY: Simon & Schuster, 1987.

For Jane Loevinger's Ego development model, see her book: *Ego Development*. San Francisco: Jossey-Bass Publishers, 1976.

## Chapter 2

Frank Tipler's book is *The Physics of Immortality*. NY: Doubleday, 1994. Additional information about cognitive dissonance can be found by reading: Festinger, L., *A Theory of Cognitive Dissonance*. Stanford, CA: Stanford University Press, 1962.

For Platonic and Aristotelian thought on God's existence see: Reinhold, M., *Plato & Aristotle*. Great Neck, NY: Barron's, 1964; and Grube, G., *Plato's Thought*. Boston, MA: Beacon, 1966.

David Hume saw cause-effect based on what he called "regularity" and "custom," not reason. See Smith, N.K. *The Philosophy of David Hume*. NY: MacMillan & Co, 1964.

Physicist George Smoot's quote on how scientists often discard their spiritual beliefs was in *Omni* magazine, March, 1994, p. 70.

## Chapter 3

For more information on science and creation see Schroeder, G.L. *Genesis and the Big Bang*. NY: Bantam, 1990 (much of my rationale for the "God Theory" argument as well as some information on scripture-science consistency was first described in this excellent book); Paul

Davies's books, *God & the New Physics.* NY: Simon & Schuster, 1984 and *The Mind of God.* NY: Simon & Schuster, 1992; Smoot, G. *Wrinkles in Time.* NY: Avon Books, 1993. Others on related topics are Einstein, A. *Relativity.* NY: Crown, 1952; Thorne, K.S. *Black Holes & Time Warps.* NY: W.W. Norton & Co., 1994; Hawking, S.H. *A Brief History of Time.* NY: Bantam, 1988; Trefil, J. *The Moment of Creation.* NY: Scribner's Sons, 1983; Weinberg, S. *The First Three Minutes.* NY: Basic Books, 1977.

To read more about Rawlinson's and Warren's excavations, as well as those of others, read Fagan, B.M., Ed. *Eyewitness to Discovery.* NY: Oxford University Press, 1997.

Hafele and Keating's test of time dilation at speeds below the speed of light is found in: "Around-the-world atomic clocks." *Science* 117:168, 1972.

Russian-born scientist George Gamov proposed the Big Bang theory in 1946 which posits the entire physical universe, including all the matter and energy–even the dimensions of space and time–was at one point an intense concentration of pure energy and burst apart at high speeds. In 1965, scientists from the Bell Telephone laboratories observed and reported on microwave background radiation, convincing most scientists of the validity of the Big Bang theory.

St. Augustine explained in *Civitas Dei* ("The City of God") that God existed outside of time.

Schroeder first described the change in reference frames and God's orientation to humans occurring in Genesis's second chapter in *Genesis and the Big Bang* (see reference above). Schroeder believes the specific verse that highlights the change is Genesis 2:7; I see the alteration in the use of "day" between Geneses 2:4 and that which precedes it as more a significant focal point of the change. Interestingly, Schroeder more recently defined his basic argument for what occurred during the "first six days," explaining the slow-moving conditions which must have been present as a consequence of "quark confinement," in *The Science of God.* NY: Broadway, 1997.

Richard Elliott Friedman's newest book is *The Hidden Book in the Bible.* San Francisco: Harper, 1998. Pierre-Paul Grasse's book *Evolution of Living Organism* (NY: Academic Press) was published in 1977.

For R.A. Clouser's ideas, see "Genesis on the origin of the human race." *Perspectives on Science & Christian Faith* 43(1):2-13, 1991.

Denton, M. *Evolution–A Theory in Crisis.* Bethesda, MD: Adler & Adler, 1985; Yockey, H.P., from "Comments on 'Let there be life: Thermodynamic reflections on biogenesis and evolution' by Avshalom Elitzer," *Journal of Theoretical Biology,* 176:349-355, 1995. Denton and Elitzer, both respected scientists assert there is absolutely no positive evidence for the existence of a "prebiotic soup" on Earth.

Information on perfect best-case scenario taken from Mills, G.C. "Presuppositions of science as related to origins." *Perspectives on Science & Christian Faith* 42(3):155-161, 1990.

For Francis Crick's comments, see p. 88 of his book *Life Itself.* NY: Simon & Schuster, 1981.

Hubert Yockey's quote is in Yockey, H.P. "A calculation of the probability of spontaneous biogenesis by information theory." *Journal of Theoretical Biology* 67:398, 1977.

Ernst Mayr's quote is from *The Growth of Biological Thought.* Cambridge, MA: Belknap Press, 1982.

Tom Kemp's quote is from his article "The reptiles that became mammals." *New Scientist* 93(1295):581, March 4, 1982.

Soren Lovtrup refutes Darwinism in his book *Darwinism – The Refutation of a Myth.* Beckingham, Kent: Croom Helm, 1987.

For more evidence of the tie between modern physics and ancient spirituality see Capra, F. *The Tao of Physics.* NY: Bantam, 1977.

## Chapter 4

S.L. Syme's work can be found in his "Social determinants of disease." *Annals of Clinical Research* 19(2):44-52, 1987; and his "Coronary artery disease." *Circulation* 76(1):112-116, 1987.

Research on contemporary interest in spirituality is from McGuire, M.B. "Health and spirituality as contemporary concerns." *ANNALS of AAPSS* 5227:144-154, May 1993.

For details on belief and health, see Pollner, M. "Divine relations, social relations, and well-being." *Journal of Health and Social Behavior* 30:92-104, 1989; and Hixson, K.A., et al. "Association between blood pressure, selected health behaviors, and religiosity in adult females." *Medicine and Science in Sports and Exercise* 29(5):S89, 1997.

Data on belief's health-protection in elderly are from Oxman, T.E., et al. "Lack of social participation or religious strength and comfort as risk factors for death after cardiac surgery in the elderly." *Psychosomatic Medicine* 57:681-689, 1995; and Zuckerman, D.M., et al. "Psychosocial predictors of mortality among the elderly poor." *American Journal of Epidemiology* 119:410-423, 1984.

Carl Jung's quote is from his "Psychotherapists or the Clergy." *Psychology and Religion – West and East.* Collected works, London: Pantheon, vol. 11, pp. 327-347, 1971.

The study on hope/optimism and breast cancer is Pettingale, K.W., et al, "Mental attitudes to cancer: An additional prognostic factor." *Lancet* March 30, 1985, p. 750.

Schmale and Iker's work found in R. Ornstein and D. Sobel, *The Healing Brain.* NY: Simon & Schuster, 1987.

For Green and Green's work on remission, see E. Green and A. Green. *Beyond Biofeedback.* NY: Dell Publishers, 1977.

Goddard's study is Goddard, N.C. "Spirituality as an integrative energy." *Journal of Advanced Nursing* 22(4):808-815, 1995.

Frankl's bestseller on the WWII deaths camps and meaning in life are in Frankl, V. *Man's Search for Meaning.* NY: Touchstone, 1984.

For general findings on connection: Berkman, L.F., and S.L. Syme. "Social networks, host resistance, and mortality." *American Journal of Epidemiology* 109:186-204, 1979; Kaplan, G.A., et al. "Social connections and mortality from all causes and from disease." *American Journal of Epidemiology* 128 (2):370-380, 1988; Seeman, T.E., and S.L. Syme. "Social networks and coronary artery disease." *Psychosomatic Medicine* 49 (4):341-354, 1987; House, J.S., et al. "The association of social relationships and activities with mortality." *American Journal of Epidemiology* 116(1):123-140, 1982; Kaplan, J.R., et al. "Social status, environment, and atherosclerosis in cynomolgus monkeys." *Arteriosclerosis* 2:359-368, 1982; Ruberman W., et al. "Psychosocial influences on mortality after myocardial infarction." *New England Journal of Medicine* 311(9): 552-559, 1984; Goodwin, J.S., et al. "The effects of marital status on stage, treatment, and survival of cancer patients." *Journal of the American Medical Association* 258:3125-3130, 1987; Pilisuk, M., and S.H. Parks. "Social support and family stress." *Marriage and Family Review* 6:137, 1983; Williams, R.B., et al. "Prognostic importance of social and economic resources among medically treated patients with angiographically documented coronary artery disease." *Journal of the American Medical Association* 267(4):520-524, 1992; Ernster, V.L., et al. "Cancer incidence by marital status." *Journal of the National Cancer Institute* 63:567-585, 1979.

Communication and connection references: Spiegel, D., et al. "Effect of psychosocial treatment on survival of patients with metastatic breast cancer." *Lancet* ii:888-891, 1989; Pennebaker, J.W., et al. "Disclosure of traumas and immune function." *Journal of Consulting and Clinical Psychology* 56:239-245, 1988; Pennebaker, J.W., and J.R. Susman. "Disclosure of traumas and psychosomatic processes." *Social Science and Medicine* 26:327, 1988. Dr. Jamie Pennebaker, now at the University of Texas, Austin, has done groundbreaking work in this area. See Pennebaker, J.W., and S.K. Beall. "Confronting a traumatic event." *Journal of Abnormal Psychology* 95 (3):274-281, 1986.

Contact and connection: Nerem, R.M., et al. "Social environment as a factor in diet-induced atherosclerosis." *Science* 208(4451):1474-1476, 1980; Schanberg, S.M., and T.M. Field. "Sensory deprivation stress and supplemental stimulation in the rat pup and preterm neonate." *Child Development* 58:1431-1447, 1987; Jourard, S.M. "An exploratory study of body-accessibility." *British Journal of Social & Clinical Psychology* 5(3):221-231, 1966.

Community and connection: Wolf, S. "Predictors of myocardial infarction over a span of 30 years in Roseto, PA." *Integrative Physiological & Behavioral Science* 27(3):246-257, 1993; Egolf, B., et al. "Featuring health risks and mortality – The Roseto effect." *American Journal of Public Health* 82 (8):1089-1092, 1992; Wolf, S., and J.G. Bruhn. *The Power of Clan.* NY: Transaction Press, 1993; Benet, S. *Abkhasians: The Long-Living People of the Caucasus.* NY: Holt, Rinehart & Winston, 1974; Benet, S. *How to Live to be 100.* NY: Dial Press, 1976.

Crisis and connection quote: see M. Scott Peck's *The Road Less Traveled.* loc. cit., Ornish, D. *Reversing Heart Disease.* NY: Ballantine, 1990. David McClelland may be one of the best research psychologists of the century. See McClelland, D.C., and C. Kirshnit. "The effect of motivational arousal through films on salivary immunoglobulin A." *Psychology and Health* 2:31-52, 1988; McClelland, D.C. "Motivational factors in health and disease." *American Psychologist* 44(4):675-683, 1989. Medalie, J.H., et al. "Angina pectoris among 10,000 men II." *American Journal of Medicine* 60(6):910-921, 1992. Siegel, B. "Love, Medicine, and Miracles." NY: Harper & Row, 1986.

For more on connection at every level, see Pert, C. *Molecules of Emotion.* NY: Simon & Schuster, 1997; Schrodinger, E. *What is Life? and Mind and Matter.* London: Cambridge University Press, 1969.

For more on type A behavior and hostility see Raymond, C. "Distrust rage may be toxic core that puts Type A person at risk." *Journal of the American Medical Association* 261:813, 1989; Friedman, M., and D. Ulmer. *Treating type A behavior and your heart.* NY: Knopf, 1984; Friedman, M., and R.H. Rosenman. *Type A Behavior and Your Heart.* NY: Fawcett, 1984; Blumenthal, J.A., et al. "Psychological correlates of hostility among patients undergoing coronary angiography." *British Journal of Medical Psychology* 60:349-355, 1987; Dembroski, T.M., et al. "Components of hostility as predictors of sudden death and myocardial infarction in the Multiple Risk Factor Intervention Trial." *Psychosomatic Medicine* 51:514-522, 1989; Dembroski, T.M. "Moving beyond Type A." *Advances: Journal of the Institute for the Advancement of Health* 1:16-26, 1984; Diamond, S., *The Double Brain.* London: Churchill Livingstone, 1972; Williams, R. *The Trusting Heart.* NY: Times Books, 1989.

For more on type C personality: LeShan, L. "Psychological states as factors in the development of malignant disease." *Journal of the National Cancer Institute* 22:1-8, 1959; Kissen, D.M., et al. "A further report on personality and psychosocial factors in lung cancer." *Annals of the New York Academy of Sciences* 164(2):535-545, 969.; Graves, P.L., et al. "Familial and psychological predictors of cancer." *Cancer Detection & Prevention* 15(1):59-64, 1991; Schaffer J.W., et al. "Family attitudes in youth as a possible precursor of cancer among physicians." *Journal of Behavioral Medicine* 5(2):143-163, 1982; Thomas, C.B., et al. "Closeness to parents and the family constellation in a prospective study of five disease states." *Johns Hopkins Medical Journal* 134:251-270, 1974; Thomas, C.B.,et al. "Family attitudes reported in youth as potential predictors of cancer." *Psychosomatic Medicine* 41:287-302, 1979.

For more information on R. Buckminster Fuller's concept of "cosmic costing," see his *Critical Path.* NY: St. Martin's Press, 1981.

For references on forgiveness and health, see Kaplan, B.H. "Social health and the forgiving heart – The type B story." *Journal of Behavioral Medicine* 15:3-14, 1992; Pettit, G.A. "Forgiveness – A teachable skill for creating and maintaining health." *New Zealand Medical Journal* 100:180-192, 1987; Strasser, J.A. "The relation of general forgiveness and forgiveness type to reported health in the elderly." Unpublished dissertation, Catholic University of America, WA, DC, 1984; Freedman, S.R., et al. "Forgiveness as an intervention goal with incest survivors." *Journal of Consulting and Clinical Psychology* 64(5):983-992, 1996; Al-Mabuk, R.H., et al. "Forgiveness education with parentally love-deprived late adolescents." *Journal of Moral Education* 24(4):427-444,1995; Trainer, M.F. "Forgiveness – Intrinsic, role-expected, expedient, in the context of divorce." Unpublished dissertation, Boston University, Boston, MA, 1981.

For references on altruism, see Novak, P. *Religion and Altruism.* Sausalito, CA: Institute of Noetic Sciences, 1992; Trout, S.S. *Born to Serve.* Alexandria, VA: Three Roses Press, 1997.

Alan Luks. *The Healing Power of Doing Good,* NY: Random House, 1992.

For more information on prayer, read Strawbridge, W.J., et al. "Frequent attendance at religious services and mortality over 28 years" *American Journal of Public Health* 87:957-961, 1997; Kark, et al. "Does religious observance promote health?" *American Journal of Public*

*Health,* 86:341-346, 1996; Byrd, R.C. "Positive therapeutic effects of intercessory prayer in a coronary care unit population." *Southern Medical Journal* 81(7):826-829, 1988; Dossey, L. *Healing Words.* NY: Harper Collins, 1993; Pearsall, P. *Making Miracles: Finding Meaning in Life's Chaos.* NY: Avon Books, 1993.

For other general references on spirituality and health, see Aldridge, D. "Is there evidence for spiritual healing?" *Advances – the Journal of Mind-Body Health* 9(4):4-21, 1993, and the many responses to it in the issues that follow; Ornstein, R., et al. *Healthy Pleasures.* NY: Addison-Wesley, 1989; Borysenko, J. *Minding the Body, Mending the Mind.* NY: Bantam Books, 1988; Pearsall, P. *Super Immunity – Master Your Emotions and Improve Your Health.* NY: McGraw-Hill, 1987; Pearsall, P. *Making Miracles.* NY: Avon Books, 1991.

## Chapter 5

Grassie, W. "Science as epic?" *Science & Spirit* 9(1):8-9, 1998.

For more about Smoot's work, see his book with Keay Davidson: Smoot G. *Wrinkles in Time.* NY: Avon Books, 1993.

See Gingerich, O., in *Science and Theology: Questions at the Interface,* (Murray Rae, et al., eds.) Edinburgh: T & T Clarke, 1994; Carter, B., "Large number of coincidences and the anthropic principle in cosmology." *Confrontation of Cosmological Theories with Observation* (S. Longair, ed.) NY: Reidel, 1974; Barrow, J.D., et al. *The Anthropic Cosmological Principle.* Oxford: Clarendon Press, 1986.

Steven Weinberg's *Dreams of a Final Theory* was published in NY by Vintage Books in 1994.

## Chapter 6:

Demographic information from U.S. Census Bureau through various sources. Bureau reports and current census information can be obtained easily on the world-wide web: < www.census.gov >.

See 1993 Youth at Risk Survey, commissioned by the Division of Adolescent and School Health at the National Center for Chronic Disease Prevention.

Victor Frankl's information on suicide from both his *Man's Search for Meaning.* NY: Touchstone, 1984, and *The Unheard Cry For Meaning.* NY: Touchstone, 1978.

Stephen Carter's book, *The Culture of Disbelief,* was published in 1994 in NY by Bantam Doubleday.

Regarding drug abuse and religiosity, researcher J.K. Cochran concluded an article on the topic, "The effects of religiosity on adolescent self-reported frequency of drug and alcohol use." (*Journal of Drug Issues* 22:91-104, 1991) by saying "given the stability and consistency of the controlling influence of religiosity on drug use, we suggest that religiosity be formally included in theories of use and that measures of religiosity be regularly included in future research on the epidemiology and etiology of use/abuse."

Maslow's quote from his *Toward a Psychology of Being.* NY: Van Nostrand, 1968. The articles on Chopra are "Lord of Immortality," in *Forbes,* April 11, 1994, and "Deepak's Instant Karma," in *Newsweek,* Oct. 20, 1997. One of Chopra's most interesting books is *The Seven Spiritual Laws of Success,* by Random House (NY: 1994). His book on aging is *Ageless Body, Timeless Mind.* NY: Harmony Books, 1993.

Dyer, Wayne. *Real Magic.* NY: HarperCollins, 1992.

Walsch, N.D. *Conversations With God* (Vol. 1, 2 & 3). NY: G.P. Putnam's Sons, 1995, ff.

Pilzer, Paul Zane. *God Wants You to Be Rich.* NY: Simon & Schuster, 1995.

Schwartz, Tony. *What Really Matters.* NY: Bantam Books, 1995.

Scott Cook's quote from "The ethics of bootstrapping," *Inc.* magazine, Sept., 1992. For more on this see *Leading with Soul* by Lee Bolman and Terrence Deal (San Francisco: Jossey-Bass Publishers, 1995) and *Spirit At Work: Discovering the Spirituality in Leadership* by Jay Conger, et al. (San Francisco: Jossey-Bass Publishers, 1994.

For more on the various religions, see Goldman, A.L. *The Search for God at Harvard.* NY: Ballantine Books, 1992; Hanh, T.N. *Living Buddha, Living Christ.* NY: Simon & Schuster, 1996; Rost, H.T.D. *The Golden Rule – A Universal Ethic.* Oxford: Ronald, 1986; Smith, H. *The World's Religions.* NY: HarperCollins, 1991.

For more on death and life see Kubler-Ross, E. *On Death and Dying.* NY: Collier, 1969; Kubler-Ross, E. *Death: The Final Stage of Growth.* NY: Touchstone, 1975; Nuland, S.B. *How We Die.* NY: Knopf, 1993; Eadie, B.J. *Embraced By The Light.* NY: Bantam Books, 1994; Fiefel, H. "Psychology and Death." *American Psychologist* 45(4): 537-543, 1990; Frankl. V. "Facing the transitoriness of human existence." *Generations – Aging and the Human Spirit* 7-10, Fall, 1990; Wren-Lewis, J. "Aftereffects of near-death experiences." *Journal of Transpersonal Psychology.* 26(2):107-115, 1994; Greyson, B. "The phenomenology of near-death experiences." *American Journal of Psychiatry* 137:1193-1195, 1980.

Additional copies of this book may be obtained
from your local bookstore or
by sending $22 per copy
plus $4 postage/handling

to:

**Hope Publishing House**
**P.O. Box 60008**
**Pasadena, CA 91116**

CA residents please add 8¼% sales tax
FAX orders to: (626) 792-2121
Telephone: (626) 792-6123
VISA/MC orders to (800) 326-2671
E-mail orders to: hopepub@loop.com
Visit our Web site: http://www.hope-pub.com